SURVIVAL IN THE WILD

SURVIVAL IN THE WILD

Cindy Buxton

COLLINS
St James's Place, London
1980

William Collins Sons and Co Ltd
London · Glasgow · Sydney · Auckland
Toronto · Johannesburg

First published 1980

Set in Compugraphic Baskerville

ISBN 0 00 216098 6

Made and Printed in Great Britain by
T. J. Press (Padstow) Ltd

To my parents
with thanks for all their encouragement,
support and most important of all,
their love

ACKNOWLEDGEMENTS

I would like to thank the following kind friends who gave me so much help and advice during my time in Africa: His Excellency the President of Zambia, Kenneth Kaunda; Bill and Thaelia Barclay; Norman Carr; Sam and Heather Fripp; Bob and Jenny Grunsell; John and Sandy Hopcraft; Wilfrid and Mairo Hopcraft; the late Ras Asserate Kassa and his family; Miene Masters; Peter and Annette Miller; Derek and Sue Petrie; David and Jenny Slater; the Zambian Game Department; Zambia Safaris Ltd; and the *Survival* team and Anglia Television for whom I was filming.

CONTENTS

LIST OF ILLUSTRATIONS

FOREWORD

I have known Cindy Buxton since she was very young and have always admired her spirit and determination. My wife and I have twice been on photographic safari with her in Africa, and I have always been impressed by her amazing resourcefulness in wild places, and her adaptability in all sorts of circumstances which would deter most people, young or old.

But it is as an ornithologist that I particularly welcome her first book, because it is rare for somebody so young to gain a notable first. Her film and studies of the shoebill, or whale-headed stork, constitute an important contribution to ornithological knowledge. Cindy's very complete documentation of this extraordinary bird, both on film and in these pages, is a remarkable achievement.

I am therefore delighted to contribute this introduction to what I hope will be the first of many accounts of her travels and wildlife filming adventures.

Peter Scott.

Slimbridge
May 1980

ONE

The Gamble

I was twenty when I first found myself alone in Africa in 1971. I had arrived from England two weeks earlier with my father and sister, and we had travelled hundreds of miles around Tanzania and Kenya, finishing up on the north east shore of Lake Rudolph, since named Lake Turkana, a wonderfully wild and barren wilderness which conforms more to one's ideas of the moon.

Then when the family left Africa for home, I stayed behind with my camera to see if I could make a wildlife film on my own. To attempt this I was prepared to risk all my resources. Nobody seemed certain that the film would actually come out, let alone whether there would be wildlife visible in the picture. I have tackled several daunting projects since, but this first one was hand picked for my first attempt. The spectacle of a million flamingos on Lake Nakuru, massed in the African sunshine, accompanied by thousands of water birds from pelicans to tiny sandpipers, with the odd hippopotamus, reasonably tame antelope and other game around the lakeside, provided the answer to any beginner's prayer. But at the time, being young and so new to that breathtaking part of the world, I felt that I was Livingstone, Van der Post, Armand Denis and Jane Goodall all rolled into one. England seemed very far away, and although I was to be securely lodged with friends, I felt rather apprehensive.

It had been arranged for me to stay with John Hopcraft,

the tireless pioneer of Nakuru conservation, whom I had met in London a year before, and who lived with his wife Sandy on a beautiful farm on the east side of the lake. Having been lent an old Peugeot, I drove myself up the Rift valley and reached John and Sandy in the evening.

Their farm, called Baharini, stretches for some miles along the lake which was bordered by dense reed beds and swamps. Behind the farm lies a wide belt of acacia forest. The place teemed with birds. The Hopcraft residence consisted of several round buildings or rondavels, of various sizes, all built of clay, timber and cement. John had been born in one of the roundavels forty years before.

Lake Nakuru is one of the smaller lakes lying in the Rift valley at 5,500 feet. It is seven miles long by four wide, and was world famous as the greatest bird spectacle in Africa. Nakuru was also the first national park in Africa set aside solely for its prolific bird life, and in 1961 two thirds of the lake were put under legal protection. Then in 1968 the whole lake and its immediate foreshore, a total of 14,000 acres, was finally and officially declared a national park. Later, in 1973, the World Wildlife Fund raised the money to purchase a protective buffer zone to the south-east. Unfortunately, the town of Nakuru, which is the third largest town in Kenya, lies at the north-east end of the lake. Factories springing up there are a constant threat to the birds, because whereas there are several rivers running into the lake, none runs out, so industrial waste and effluent are trapped and cause pollution.

During my first week at Nakuru I spent many hours near the lake keeping quiet and just watching and noting. On John's advice I finally set up a total of four hides. The first was on the south shore by the mouth of the Nderit River. This was a fascinating place, as every morning the flamingos and other birds would come to the mouth of the river and wash themselves in the fresh water. They would spend about an hour ducking under the water and preening to clean the soda off

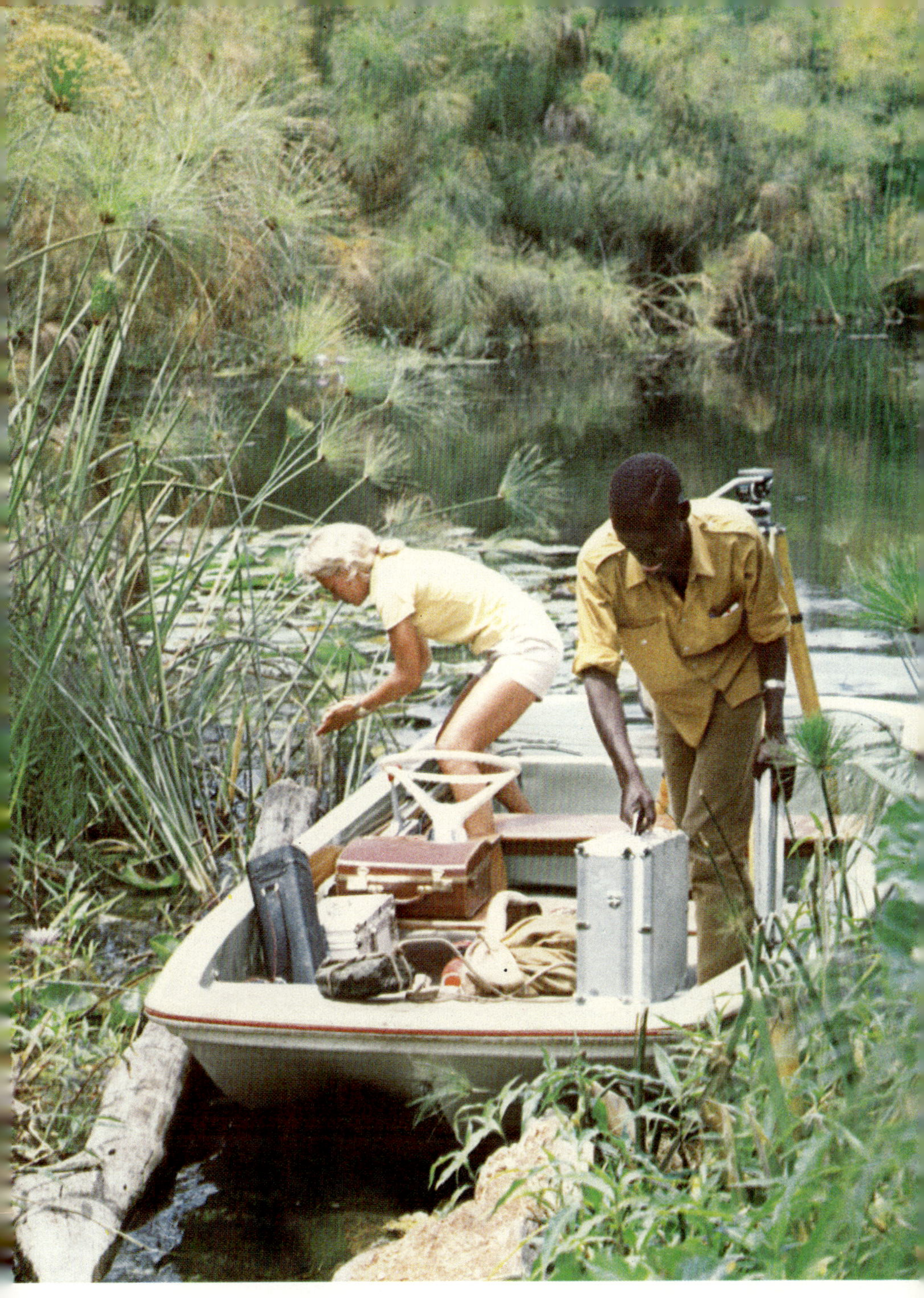

The floating worlds of Naivasha.

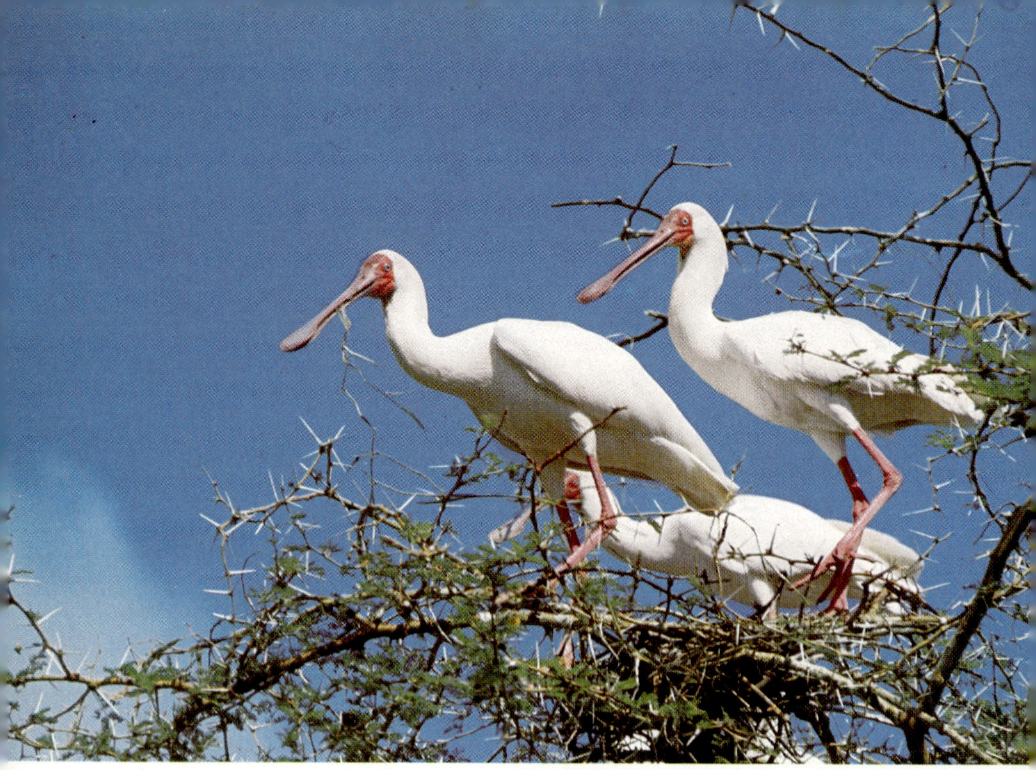

African Spoonbills.

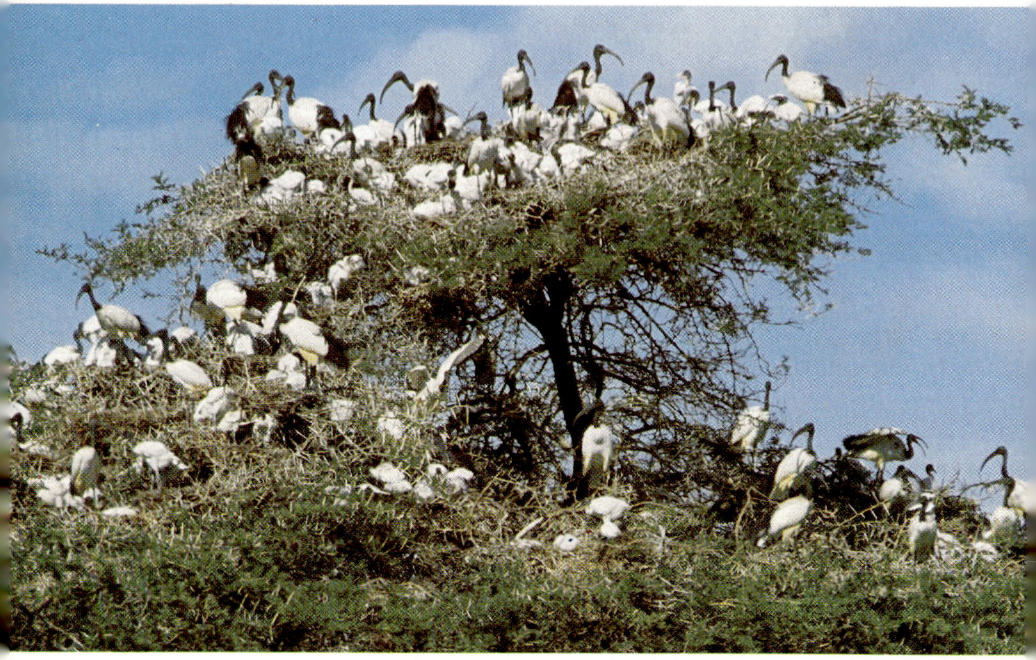

Colony of sacred ibis.

their feathers. Then after a clean up they would be ready for the day's feeding in the thick soup of the lake. The soda, or sodium carbonate, is present in heavy concentrations in the water, in some places forming almost solid deposits. I was told that its presence derives from the volcanic ash which seeps into the water.

I made the second hide on top of some old water troughs. Years before the level of the lake had been lower, and the farmer who then owned the land had built these troughs for his cattle. After several successive years of torrential rains, the lake rose and the troughs, flooded out, became excellent perches on which the birds preened themselves or basked in the sun.

I built my hide on the end trough so that I was about thirty yards out in the lake and very close to the birds. I was able to get some lovely shots of the cormorants who sat only a few feet from me, and of the greater flamingos feeding close by. In deeper water they would upend themselves, using their legs as paddles to keep their heads on the bottom. With their beaks they filter the mud and water, catching the algae as it passes through. The lesser flamingos paddle in shallower water and shift their feet around in the mud to stir up the bottom.

I had to be inside the hide in darkness and settled in before sunrise, and then stay there until it was dark again, if the birds and animals were to be totally unaware of my presence. This meant that I was sometimes in the hide for twelve hours or more at a stretch. I got fearful backache from crouching down in such a tiny space.

The third hide consisted of an old water tank. I cut a circular hole in one end with a lid fitted over the top. Four small windows were cut around the top of the tank, and sacking curtains made to fit. John and I transported this extraordinary object down to the lake shore and with several game guards dug a large hole and sank the drum up to the level of the window. We had great difficulty in keeping the hide down in the hole as the water level was only a few inches below ground and the water pressure forced it up, so we half filled the tank with sand from the lake shore to weigh it down. This was fine, except that it gave me the minimum space possible in which to film. It was by far the most uncomfortable hide of the four and became extremely hot in the heat of the day. I could have fried an egg on the roof. But in the end it was worth it because I was able to film, at their eye level, many of the tiny wading birds that run about on the margin of the lake.

I had several problems with this hide. Once a tourist walked up to the hide, opened the lid and threw in an empty beer can which narrowly missed my head. The poor man saw a woman curled up at the bottom of the bin, and went deathly pale, thinking no doubt that I was a missing corpse.

On another occasion, I had crept into this underground bin before sunrise and during the heat of the day, when all the wildlife had sought shelter from the overhead sun to sleep, I had curled up in the bottom of my tank to snooze. At about three o'clock, very slowly and carefully I drew back one of the curtains to see what was going on outside. To my utter amazement all I could perceive was something like a fat, white, hairy leg. I knew of no bird, not even a prehistoric marabou, that looked like this. Realizing that the leg must belong to some unsuspecting tourist, I could think of no other course than to say in stern and measured tones 'Would you kindly remove yourself?' It is surprising I suppose that the portly intruder did not die of shock, hearing voices from down under in the heart of darkest Africa. But he took flight in an instant, and when I raised the lid he was floundering towards the shoreline.

The last hide was a floating affair so that I could sail out into the middle of the lake to film flamingos and other birds in close-up. It was basically a square wooden platform with a hole cut in the middle so that I could stand in it and wade on the bottom of the lake. Under the platform were blocks of polystyrene which kept it afloat, and on top was my hide. The whole contraption was just light enough for me to lift and carry down to the lake.

The lake was at that time very shallow, with an average depth of about three feet, but of course there were deep holes and I seemed to be adept at finding them and suddenly sinking out of my depth, eventually to surface again inside the hide coughing and spluttering and soaked through in the soda-saturated water, which burns the skin if it is not washed off in fresh water as soon as possible.

I was once filming a large group of flamingos out in the middle of the lake when I heard an ominous grunt just outside the hide. As I was hundreds of yards from the shore it could hardly be a pig. I peeped nervously out of the window and my heart stopped when I saw a huge hippo that had surfaced literally three feet away. This really shook me. Here was I, the new girl from England, up to my armpits in water and staring at a hippo within touching distance. We stared at each other, eyeball to eyeball, for a few long seconds, and then the hippo quietly submerged with a snort and a huff and disappeared from view.

With my raft I was able to get right up to the flamingos which were displaying out in the middle of the lake. They formed into large groups and the lesser flamingos straightened their necks and fluffed out their pink feathers in unison. Suddenly they would all bow their heads as though their necks had broken.

The greater flamingos display in a different way, though they often group with the lesser flamingos. They also straighten their necks and fluff out their neck feathers, but then they twist their heads from side to side with their beaks raised aloft. They make a different noise during display than at any other time, and when they are in large groups the din is deafening.

I was also able to float out to the cormorant colonies which were in dead trees that were once above the level of the lake. I filmed the adults building their nests and feeding their young. The young put their entire heads down into the throats of the parents to pick out the partially digested fish. I also got many other birds swimming around the lake, including the pelicans in their communal fishing formation. They swim in a tight U and then all submerge their heads together, closing the gap in the U and trapping the fish in the centre.

Nakuru was my first attempt at filming and of course I made terrible mistakes which threw me into fits of depression. Once I sent a few thousand feet of film back to *Survival* in London, and waited for the usual report. I got a shock when I received it, since the whole lot had been totally blank. The most evil cynics seemed to have been proved right for I had accidentally knocked on the fader of my little wind-up camera without noticing.

Another time a report came back that although the film itself was fine there was a thin white line running down the left hand side all the way through, and therefore all the footage was useless. The filter-holder had fallen out and once more I had failed to notice it. I try never to make the same mistakes twice.

Towards the end of March, I flew to Lake Natron with Leslie Brown, world famous ornithologist and author, to see an incredible sight, the lesser flamingos at their breeding colony. Lake Natron is bright red with brilliant white stripes slashed across it. The red is caused by the algae, and the white streaks are high concentrations of soda. Natron is a very big lake with mountains and steep escarpments on all sides except to the north, where a flat plain extends to the next lake, Magadi. The flamingos build their nests about a mile out into Lake Natron, which protects them from predators. It is impossible to walk out, as the lake bed is soft and the soda so strong that if it touches the skin it can cause severe burns. Even the marabou storks, one of the flamingos' enemies, do not bother to fly out to the nesting colonies to eat the eggs and the young chicks, because it is so unbearably hot and airless.

I remember a remarkable symptom of the fierce conditions in the centre of Natron. When we made our flight I was piloting the Cessna while Leslie Brown was observing and taking photographs of the colony. We had had the door of the aircraft removed to facilitate photography and every time I banked at a few hundred feet the hot air wafted into the cabin as if we had stirred up a crackling log fire at home.

Later, back at Nakuru, I was brought a twelve foot python by a local boy, which I thought I might use in the film. The Africans at Baharini watched in amazement as I carried the huge snake coiled around my waist, holding on to its head. I must have appeared quite mad, but it was the most comfortable way to carry it both for me and the snake. The python was not very successful in his acting career but he did give me many hours of entertainment.

One day I took him into open country and gently lifted him out of the sack in the back of the car. I wanted to film him swimming in one of the fresh water pools around the lake. I let him out and put him down by the car, and he promptly wriggled under it. After a while, I peered under the car to find out what he was up to. All I could see was the end of his tail. He had coiled himself round the engine for extra warmth.

I groaned and sat down to contemplate how on earth I was going to get the python out. I tried to uncoil him from inside the engine, but this had no effect at all, because his muscles were incredibly strong and no matter how much I pulled he would not move an inch. Finally I lay on my back under the car and worked from there. It took nearly two hours to unravel this snake from the engine. I had not yet set up any records in Africa, but I suppose I may have been the first English girl to unwind a python from the engine of a motor car.

The year 1971 was very dry and the land got steadily more burnt up until fires started on all the farms. Baharini was no exception and we had one terrible week when there were nine fires in seven days. If I was around I would help John, Sandy and the farm hands to put out the blaze with wet sacks. At last, several months later, the rains came.

Those first rains brought tragedy to the lake. Early one morning I found several hundred marabou storks gathered in large groups feeding on the shore line. I got out of my car and walked up to the water's edge. Literally thousands of dead tilapia fish were floating in the shallows and washing gently onto the shore. I walked for several hundred yards and saw thousands more dead fish. I got hold of the park warden and some game wardens, and we all examined the fish but could not conceive why they had died. John took several sample fish and had them specially packed and sent away to laboratories to be analysed: we learnt eventually that the first torrential rains had flooded the streets of Nakuru town and swept the contents of the drains into the lake. The filth of the town and the chemicals from the factories had been too much for the wretched tilapia.

The Hopcrafts' house at Baharini was also flooded out at that time. Sandy was then rearing six small and fluffy Egyptian geese. The young goslings were tame and would often waddle through the house. Sandy and I were in the sitting-room when I suddenly noticed a huge puddle forming in the next room. In less than a minute the puddle turned into a river which gushed through the kitchen, the study and the sitting-room. All of a sudden six baby goslings came proudly sailing through the back door and into the room, cheeping with delight as they swam round the sofa and armchairs, under the big table, and out through the door to the front lawn.

During my stay I had kept a sharp eye out for marabou storks killing and eating flamingos. For the last few weeks I devoted early mornings and late evenings in an attempt to get this rare event on film, because I had heard this grisly scene described but it had never been filmed. Every morning I would be in the park before sunrise, and choosing a few marabous, would follow them until mid-morning, when they leave the lake and go and sit in the grass until the heat of the day is over.

In the end I managed to film three separate killings. The last time the low morning sun was behind me and illuminated the beautiful glowing pink of the flamingos. The marabou storks would take off and fly high over the solid mass of flamingos, picking out just one unfortunate bird and gliding for it. Nearly always the first pounce was successful. The stork would grab the flamingo in its beak, crush the head and shake it to death in a few seconds. When the flamingo was dead the marabou pulled it to pieces, and then the other storks joined in, often fighting off the first one and stealing the kill. The rest of the flamingos, seeing that the marabous had got what they wanted, would once again settle down, quite unconcerned. The flamingos seemed able to sense whether the marabous were on the hunt for food or merely having a quiet stroll around the shore.

Once though, I filmed a marabou which missed on the first pounce. The stork selects a single bird, and in this instance it gave chase. Having escaped once, the poor flamingo ran straight into the thick crowd of its fellows, who thereupon parted to make way for the pursuit. The stork gave chase for several hundred yards and finally caught up with its pathetic prey, crushing its head. The rest of the flamingos moved away and settled down again to feed as if nothing had happened.

I realize that these natural stories sound sad, or may cause dismay when read, but I found that in the wild when one is almost integrated with the action, the ways of nature seem inevitable and one's overwhelming purpose is to record them for the enlightenment of all those who are interested.

In due course I secured all the film that I could of Nakuru. The time came for dismantling the hides, packing up my equipment, saying goodbye to the kind Hopcrafts, and making my way back to London, huddled in my seat on the plane. I say huddled, because I was in a state of near panic. One of the problems of filming in the wild is that you can never see what you have done, and have to rely on reports from other people. When you get home it is too late to make amends. Apart from a few encouraging signals from base, that there were 'some nice sequences', I had no idea whether I had done enough to complete a half-hour film. If I had failed, my resources were exhausted, and it would be a case, in next to no time, of becoming a shop girl behind the counter in a department store.

I arrived in the *Survival* office in a state of frozen apprehension to see the master of wildlife programme writers, Colin Willock, and felt somehow disembodied, watching myself knock on the door and listen to the verdict. Was this to be the end of my life-long ambition to travel, to film and to lead a life of adventure?

Colin greeted me with an air of confidence and encouragement 'I think we have some good stuff here and it should make a very nice film . . .'

I slumped into a chair as waves of relief swept over me. So this, after all, was not to be the end, but the beginning.

TWO

A Floating World

With the money I was paid for the flamingo film, I was able to buy a ticket to Kenya and a more up-to-date Bolex camera which one did not have to wind. There was even some money left to buy a Land-Rover. I think this is what is called ploughing back profits, but to me it was like ploughing in precious pocket money.

My original intention had been to film the malachite kingfishers on Lake Nakuru, but I ended up at Lake Naivasha in amongst the papyrus swamps and lagoons. The malachites had rivals and the woodland kingfishers turned out to be the stars. I spent at least a month exploring the thirty square miles of Lake Naivasha looking for a suitable location, a site which was quiet, peaceful, undisturbed and beautiful. Eventually, I found exactly what the doctor ordered.

Lake Naivasha is sixty miles north of Nairobi in the Rift valley on the way to Nakuru, at 6,000 feet the highest of all the Rift lakes. It is fresh water whereas all the others are saline. The lake was created by a volcano, Longenot, which erupted thousands of years ago spilling lava into the valley and damming up part of it, thus creating a beautiful lake to the north. Underground rivers run out beneath the strata, so that the lake remains clear and pleasantly fresh.

Huge floating islands of papyrus drift about, forming beautiful lagoons within. Aquatic life thrives in profusion and the native tilapia fish and the American black bass are the most numerous. The good life and the fishing attracts large colonies of water birds, particularly egrets, cormorants and fish eagles. Naivasha is the greatest place in the Rift for fish eagles.

During my four months stay at Naivasha I stayed with Wilfrid Hopcraft and his wife Mairo. He is John Hopcraft's uncle, and owns a beautiful 7,000 acre farm right on the northern edge of the lake. It is a wonderfully peaceful place. The Hopcrafts have four children, three daughters and a son, Ricky. Ricky was a professional hunter, but when not away hunting, helped his father with the running of the farm, and certainly helped me on the lake.

The view from the house was breathtaking. A private lagoon at the bottom of the cliff was cut off from the rest of the lake by a mass of papyrus up to a mile thick, and beyond this were six miles of shimmering water to the distant shore.

I asked the Hopcrafts if they could find me a young African who would work for me and help carry all my equipment. Mairo, within a few days, found Ndungu, the son of her cook. Ndungu was a Kikuyu aged about twenty, strong, friendly and with virtually no English. However, we got on well and to my relief he began to enjoy his work and grew more and more interested in the birds and the filming. After a short time he was able to put up some of my hides, observe at nests, build any contraption that I needed, and in due course started paddling me around the lagoons.

To the east the uplands rise gently to the great escarpment and the Aberdare mountains, which were sometimes shrouded in clouds. All about us were the cries of water birds, the singing of smaller species in the scrub and the barking of antelope beyond the garden.

One evening we heard a strange noise outside coming from the lake shore. The night was bright with a full moon. We walked swiftly to the cliff edge and looked over. We saw the most amazing sight, which held our attention in total silence for almost half an hour. Below were three adult hippos, two males and a female. The males were fighting for the female, which stood silently aside watching the fun. The two males really went for each other charging, biting, bellowing and squealing at the top of their voices. The squealing was strangely high-pitched for such large animals. Finally the two males drew apart, no doubt from exhaustion, and simply glowered at each other.

One of them, presumably the loser, then turned round and started to walk morosely back to the lake. Just as he reached the edge of the water the other male broke into a gallop and charged at full speed, hitting his adversary sideways-on. This made him topple over, with a huge splash as he hit the water. The battle then appeared to be over, and the victor strolled down to the lake with the female by his side.

Having selected my lagoon, I now needed a boat of my own, and it had to be wide enough to take my tripod. I first borrowed the Hopcrafts' rowing boat which proved wonderful for rowing around the lagoons, and from which to observe all the birds, but it was too unstable for filming and not wide enough. I finally borrowed a boat which had a 20 h.p. engine, which proved to be perfect for the job.

And so I settled down to several months of hard filming in the lagoon. Lake Naivasha, although very beautiful and peaceful, is not just roses and sunshine for the wildlife photographer. A permanent battle goes on with the local fishermen who are allowed to lay down their nets out in the open lake, but not in the lagoons. But they always lay them in the lagoons when no one is looking.

Early one morning when I was paddling around, I came across two fishermen hauling up their nets. Since they were going to wreck my filming prospects for the day I was desperate and decided to take a tough line. I therefore asked them to get their nets and themselves out of the lagoon within an hour or I would report them to the authorities. I expected to be capsized and ducked in the water, but amazingly they cleared out straightaway.

That afternoon I came across a darter, a bird like a cormorant with a long thin neck, which had obviously been diving for fish. It had swum straight into a fishing net and had got its beak hopelessly entangled. Many birds drown this way, unable to surface again. Some manage to break away from the net but their beaks remain tied up with strands and they eventually die from starvation. It is pitiful to see the birds struggling to escape, with virtually no hope of success. I tried for hours to catch this darter and untie the nylon strands around its beak, but it would not let me get close enough. Unless it managed eventually to rub off the nylon the poor bird was doomed to die within a few days.

During the four months it took me to finish the kingfisher film I learned much about the lake and its bird life. The north side is nearly all imprisoned by the vast floating islands of papyrus, some a mile wide. This prevents access by most of the boats. Thus the birds and other wildlife flourish.

Papyrus is a sort of giant sedge, and is supposed to be the bulrush in which the infant Moses was found. The papyrus islands both protect the birds and provide nesting places for numerous species. In between these massive walls of papyrus are the most beautiful placid lagoons, carpeted with purple flowering lily-pads. Here is a true bird-watcher's paradise. Just sitting in the boat for only a short while, one could see the widest variety of water birds. In the papyrus are three or four species of egret, several sorts of heron – goliath, grey, purple, night, squacco, green-backed, and so on. Purple gallinules make raucous sounds inside the papyrus, whilst outside pelicans sail sedately amongst the lilies.

On the lily-pads many nimble and sure-footed smaller birds dance from leaf to leaf. First there is the enchanting lily-trotter, or African jacana. These white and chestnut water birds carry their tiny young from pad to pad gripped firmly under one wing. There are a great many visiting waders during the migration, ruffs and reeves, and especially sandpipers – green, wood, common and marsh. And of course greenshanks, which seem to penetrate right across Africa on migration – I always wondered if they had just flown from home in Norfolk.

Above the lilies and the glinting surface of the clear water soar and hover the true fishermen, the fish eagles, the terns and the kingfishers. This was the rich panorama of birds that I found when I first glided through the papyrus and found the beautiful lagoon not far out from the northern shore.

The goliath heron was a favourite of mine and I spent many an enjoyable hour filming and watching him. The goliath is about five feet high and is a superb fisherman. He stalks about the lagoons very slowly and quietly, keeping a sharp eye out for passing prey. Suddenly he pounces and grabs a large tilapia in his beak, walks back to the shore, beats the fish to death on some solid object and then sedately swallows it whole. You can see clearly the large fish slowly being drawn down his long neck.

One goliath had one major irritant, the lovely fish eagle, which regularly tried to steal the fish the heron had just caught. The enemy swooped low and dive-bombed the goliath, giving him such a fright that he would often drop the fish which the fish eagle would grab in a flash. Several times I saw this happen, but once the fish eagle was seconds too late. The goliath had swallowed the fish.

But on another day, when I had no camera with me, the goliath decided he had had enough. The heron had just caught a large fish and walked over to the shore to deal with the wriggling prey. Suddenly the eagle came circling over at low altitude and did his best to frighten the heron. This time the goliath waited until the fish eagle landed nearby and then, dropping the fish on the ground, actually charged the eagle. A battle broke out. Although the eagle is much shorter than the goliath heron, he has sharp weapons in his beak and talons. The goliath for his defence had his tall stature and long beak. The goliath thrust its head and neck at the eagle to try to stab, while the eagle tried to claw at the heron with its talons. Suddenly the goliath grabbed hold of the fish eagle's back and literally ducked it under water. When the rather demoralized eagle surfaced it used its wings to paddle itself to a dead branch in the lagoon, where it sat for several hours drying itself in the sun. The goliath stalked away, picked up its fish and swallowed it. But it was not long before the eagle was back on the attack once more, giving the poor heron the usual treatment.

Some filming I did later was at a fish eagle's nest. This was at the top of a very high tree, but by climbing up a steep and rocky precipice I could get to the level of the next. Time was short and I wanted to get some film of the parent birds catching fish. So for once I told Ndungu to go out in the boat and fish for half an hour each morning. The fish that he caught I threw back into the lagoon, much to his horror, making sure that the fish eagles saw what was going on. The dead fish floated just below the surface of the water and were an easy target for the birds. Back behind my camera I would sit and wait, and after a short while the eagles, one at a time, would come planing down and skim along the surface of the lagoon and grab the dead fish in their talons.

The parents visited the nest frequently with the fish they had just caught. At the beginning, when the young were still quite small, the parents would tear the fish up into strips so that the young could eat it. Later on the young were given whole fish which they had to learn to tear up themselves.

Soon the young were old enough to leave the nest but they stayed near their parents for a while learning how to fish and look after themselves. It took them some time before they could even call properly. During the time when they are still unable to make the famous fish eagle call, visitors hearing the extraordinary squawk they make are sometimes fooled into thinking that it is some new species of bird.

Really lovely birds were the woodland kingfishers. While I had been filming malachites, I had sent Ndungu out in search of a woodland kingfisher's nest. One day when I was paddling round the lagoon in pursuit of a malachite which I wanted to film diving for fish, I had noticed a woodland flying up to a dead tree standing in the middle of the lagoon. The bird had disappeared into the trunk of the tree and then reappeared. So I asked Ndungu to climb another tree that looked over the lagoon and to sit and watch the dead tree and report back in the evening. He finally saw the woodland kingfisher go into the dead tree several times during the day, and he thought there must be a nest there. I went to check myself one day and sat amongst the papyrus. I saw the woodland go into a little hole half way up the trunk of the dead tree and stay there for some time. At the end of the day I paddled up and with a torch looked inside the hole, and sure enough there were three small white eggs.

I spent several weeks filming this pair of kingfishers rearing their young. One of the adult birds would sit on the eggs while the other went off in search of food. Having fed, they would change over nest duty while the mate flew off to fish. After ten days the eggs hatched out and three tiny, bald woodland chicks sat squeaking at the bottom of the hole in the tree trunk. The parents became frantically busy hunting for enough food to feed their young and themselves. The chicks had tiny white dots at the very end of their beaks which were evidently guide marks for the parents to stuff the food down their throats in the darkness of the hole. Dragonflies and tree-frogs were in most demand, with various grubs for the second course.

For three weeks the parents kept up a permanent flow of goodies, occasionally stopping to feed themselves. I would sit hidden in amongst the papyrus in my boat about thirty feet from the nest. After one month the chicks were mature enough to leave the nest but they did not go far. I was surprised when I realized that the adult birds had mated again and the female after a short time returned to the same dead tree and, using the same hole, laid three more eggs. While all this was going on I had been absorbed with the main objective which was to secure the first film on the tiny brilliant and sparkling malachite kingfishers.

It did not take me long to find the first malachite nest because it was in a rubbish pit in the Hopcrafts' garden. Having found the nest and discovered two babies in residence, I started to dig a hole very cautiously at the back of the nest, so that I could subsequently open it up and see the young inside. Digging the hole was slow work because the parents were busy feeding the young and my presence might have upset them. Therefore I could only dig while the parents were away fishing, and as soon as they turned up I would stop work. Consequently it took me four days before I could finally cut my way into the back of the nest. I then placed glass at the back of the nest, finally covering the whole with a piece of cardboard and covering that with soil to block out the light.

I found seven malachite nests, all of which either had two eggs or two young chicks. I watched them all carefully to determine what stage they had reached. Three nests had two chicks each and in these I excavated and opened up the back. I was anxious to film the young being fed by the adult birds, and I also wanted to watch them grow and finally film them leaving their nests.

I chose one of the three nests to film the parents feeding. Lacking any light I used a primitive form of reflector. I got a large piece of cardboard and covered it with silver foil, and by facing it towards the sun the reflection would shine down into the nest. All the time I had to be careful of the parent birds because I was unsure how they would react. For two days I managed to film the inside of the nest with the young being

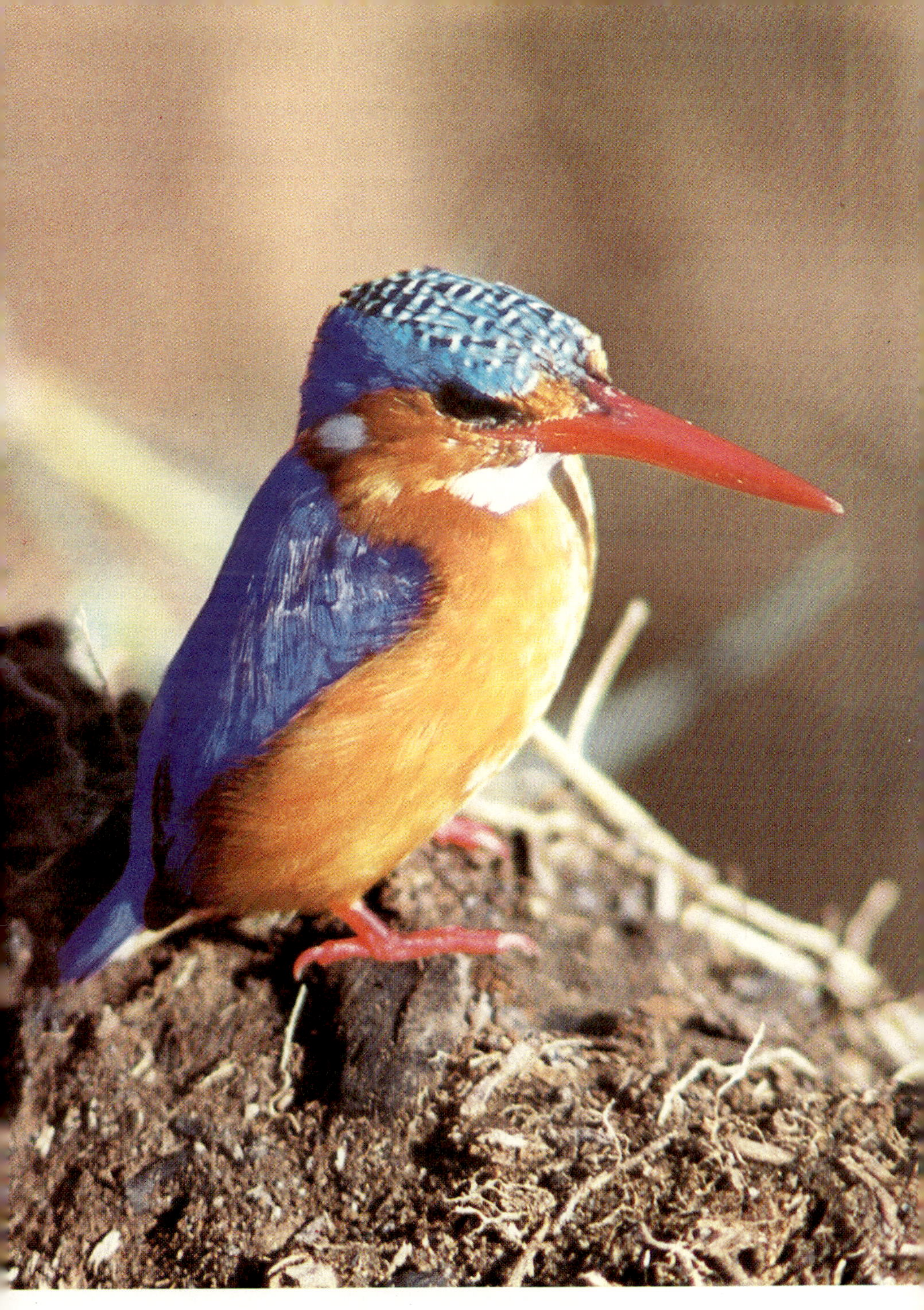

Malachite Kingfisher.

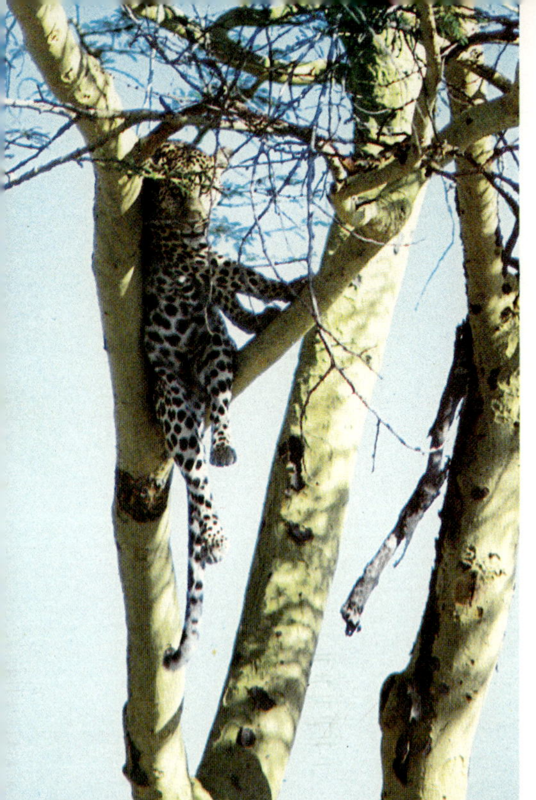

Watchful leopard.

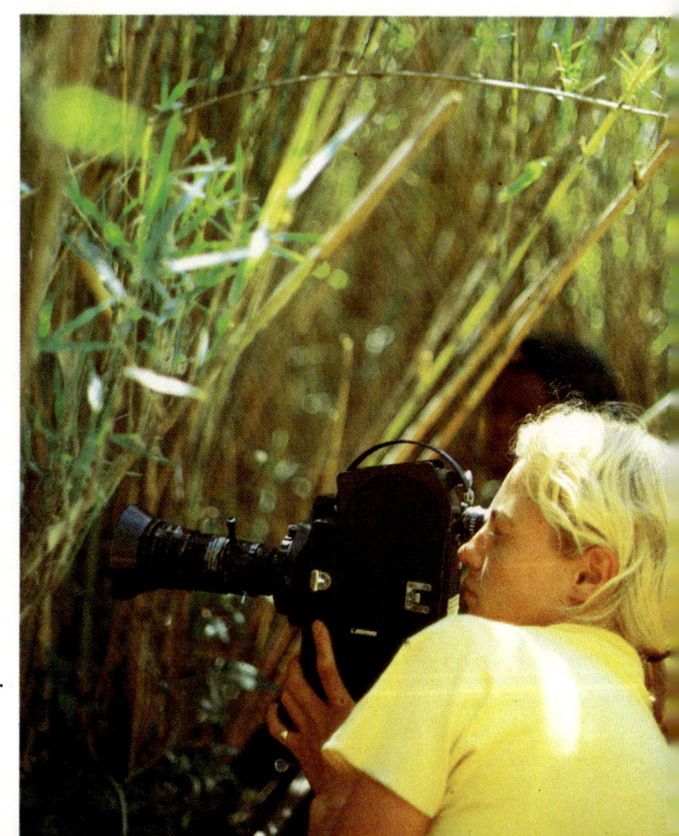

In the papyrus swamps.

fed by the parents. They obviously did not feel happy about the strong light at the back of the nest, and were reluctant to come right in. After the second day I decided to close up the hole as I feared that the parents might desert their young if I did not leave them alone.

The other thing that I very much wanted to film was the young malachites leaving their nest. Out of the seven nests I missed the departure of the chicks four times. I would sit in front of these nests all day watching for the young to come out. It was not until one morning about six, when the sun was just rising, that I saw the young malachites from one of the three remaining nests leave and fly off.

Six o'clock in the morning is too early to film, so I just had to think of a way to catch the young coming out later in the day. I got hold of a long straight stick and padded it well at one end. One of the nests which I had already opened at the back housed two chicks that were almost ready to leave, so one morning I got Ndungu to prod the chicks, very gently, along the tunnel until they appeared at the entrance. I was hoping that they might fly up on to a branch of a nearby tree and be joined by their parents, but they just sat in front of their tunnel looking rather dazed and sulky.

By June I had got everything I could on kingfishers, and I had to return to England to deliver the film footage by a certain date. I finally got myself on a flight and sank back into my seat once more wondering how long it would be before I could get back to Africa again. It turned out to be not so long, but this time to a land in many ways much stranger than Kenya.

THREE

The Edge of the Abyss

Almost to my astonishment the *Survival* organization had now purchased my first two films, from Nakuru and Naivasha, and my destiny seemed to be confirmed when I was asked if I would go to Ethiopia to join a film expedition to the Simien Mountains.

The Simiens are a vast mass of volcanic rock in the northern part of Ethiopia, which have become eroded by time and weather into the most spectacular escarpments and pinnacles in the world. The country is so steep and stark that there are no roads at all, only the most precipitous mule tracks. Comparatively few Europeans have ever been there except to visit isolated villages on the more remote table tops in the mountains. Weird varieties of plants occur, including giant lobelias fifteen feet high, and some unique animals, the walia ibex for instance. Anglia had made several *Survival* films in Ethiopia, but the organization had never yet penetrated into the skies and clouds of the Simien Mountains, so the opportunity was exciting.

The operation would involve living in tents for up to four months in the mountains at an altitude of about fourteen thousand feet. Complex preparations had to be made. At that altitude the nights are bitterly cold. Special bags, tents and clothing would have to be taken. John Buxton, a cousin, and an experienced wildlife cameraman, was asked by *Survival* to lead the expedition because he had had previous experience in the mountains.

When everything was ready we left Heathrow in the evening and landed at Addis Ababa next morning. With me were two other members of the expedition, Lizzie Bagge, cook and friend from Norfolk, and Robin Veitch who was dealing with the administration. John Buxton was due to fly out and join us a week later.

We hired two mini-buses with drivers and finally left Addis with everything on board at half-past-six in the morning on our 350-mile journey to Bahar Dar.

The first day's journey was a long, tiring and dusty drive. The tarmac was soon left behind, and the dust and the smells told us that we were once more back in the real Africa. One could compare the Ethiopian countryside with Kenya, and Ethiopia seemed more spacious, the population more dispersed, and the distances between each tiny village far greater. Sadly the Ethiopian countryside lacked wild animals. The only creatures we were likely to see were donkeys, camels, horses and a few mules.

The second day took us from Bahar Dar to Gondar, a mere ninety miles. But we stopped on several occasions to photograph birds, particularly the carmine bee-eaters and scarlet-breasted rollers, as well as yellow-billed storks, black-headed herons, saddle-billed storks and vultures. When we finally reached Gondar, John and Robin went off to pay a few official visits, so Lizzie and I took a look around the town.

On Sunday John and I left the hotel at half-past-six in the morning so that we could go ahead of the rest of the party and perhaps do some filming on the way. We travelled to Debarek, almost our final destination by road, and then went on through the town to the Wolkefit Pass which is over one of the escarpments of the Simien Mountains.

By the afternoon we all met up and the party was joined by a young man called Hugh Smith from New Zealand.

The next morning at ten o'clock, forty mules and twenty muleteers arrived at our camp. For a few hours we argued furiously with the muleteers about the price of a mule per day. Everyone seemed to enjoy arguing and even when everything had been settled they all continued to hang about yelling at each other. It took us two more days to reach our destination of Geech.

An hour before darkness we arrived at the Simien National Park at Geech. It was marvellous to be there after two hard days riding and climbing in very rough and dusty conditions. Now at about thirteen thousand feet we were still huffing and puffing.

It seemed uncanny at the time, but the very first animal we saw within five minutes of our arrival was the very rare Simien fox. We all concluded that this was a good omen, although our cameras were at the time on the back of one of the mules.

After this excitement we had tea with the park warden, Herr Muller, discussed the film and asked about the best places to find the walia ibex, gelada baboons and the lammergeyer. We decided in the end to continue up to the highest peak at Chenek, not much below 15,000 feet, so that we could slowly film our way back down the mountains for the next two to three months. Muller very kindly lent us a small tukal, or round hut, in which we could house the unwanted equipment while we went on up to Chenek.

The situation at Geech was dramatic. The panorama of precipices, peaks and plains so far below were almost invisible. One might have been sitting on a cloud. There was the feeling of being separated from the world below, and although we were all feeling the altitude acutely and were very short of breath, the high peaks and horizons were so compelling that we were determined to climb even higher.

We started off on the final leg to Chenek at a reasonable hour, John and I in the lead with our cameras and the main party strung out behind us. It was a pleasant climb but hard on the lungs. It took us about four hours over the peaks and down into valleys. There was not a cloud in the sky and although the air was cool and the wind was often cold, the sun at this height burnt us all badly.

We saw kites, augur buzzards and many thick-billed and fan-tailed ravens, as well as several lammergeyers or bearded vultures. Finally we stumbled into Chenek in the middle of the afternoon, carrying a letter from Muller to the head game guard which asked him to allow us the use of the tukal. He was called Atu Abebe and he became a friend for life. He went out of his way to assist us in every way possible.

It was remarkable what we got used to. The night at 14,000 feet is freezing cold and one yearns for the first sunlight to reach the camp. But an hour or so later the sunlight is even less kind. The thin, clear mountain air allows the sun's ultra-violet rays to penetrate unfiltered and the result is skin burned even through one's clothing.

From the camp we looked out from a fearsome ridge which commands the incredible abyss of Geech. Apparently the yawning spectacle exceeds in magnitude the Grand Canyon. All around are the tortured consequences of millions of years of erosion on the gigantic block of lava that welled out of the earth and formed the Simiens.

Because of the scale of our undertaking and the pressure on our resources, there was no time to admire the view and we got down to work as soon as we had recovered our breath. We concentrated at once on the birds and animals we had come to film.

There was an encouraging amount of wildlife around the camp, and the gelada baboons in particular were a source of constant amusement. They are found in large groups, or troops. While filming near Chenek we engaged one troop of over a hundred and fifty. The adult males are massive creatures with manes like a lion. They have long, glossy, grey coats that look as if they have been washed with an expensive shampoo. The fur flutters freely in the wind.

The females are half the size of the males, much the same

in colour, but lack the splendid mane. The young are very amusing. They take a great delight in playing games and at times they appear to get very rough. They love to somersault, pull each other's tails and engage in wrestling bouts, finally jumping over the cliff edge to a ledge below. In one large party where I watched the young, there was a steep bare earth slide, and they would scamper up to the top and then jump and somersault all the way down, squealing with delight. As soon as they reached the bottom they would scamper back up to the top again for another go.

The adults were more reserved. A female would usually soothe the male by searching his coat and mane for ticks. After a long session of grooming the male, if he felt so inclined, would repay the lady's kindness by searching her coat. Occasionally two male baboons would have a fierce fight, uttering low barks and screams. When you spot baboons they usually see you at the same time and make a sort of snort to alert the rest of the troop. They shape their mouths into an oval and hoot fiercely, the males drawing back the upper lip over pink gums and snarling a warning. We never managed to achieve any serious filming of the baboons at Chenek. Later, at Geech and Sankabar, they proved more accommodating.

There are two species of Simien rat, one large and the other small. They are delightful creatures. I managed to stalk them, getting as close as twenty-five feet which gave me some nice intimate shots. In some ways they behave like rabbits, especially when they are feeding. They tear off a piece of grass and, clutching it tightly between their tiny paws, quickly shovel it into their mouths, chewing frantically. When alerted they stand as high as they can, quite motionless, listening intently. If they do not like what they hear or see, they disappear in a flash down their holes. Their greatest enemy is the augur buzzard which delights in a Simien rat for its main course. A rat is first aware of the buzzard when its shadow moves ominously over the ground, and several times I saw rats dart back into their holes as the shadow of a harmless raven floated by. The rat's alarm system is simple. The first few to spot a shadow send out a high, piercing squeak to warn all the colony to take cover at once.

We all enjoyed our stay at Chenek and were cosy and warm in our tukal. We ate our meals inside. It had a small wood stove in it and every night Hugh would get the stove going to keep us warm. At night the temperature dropped to well below freezing.

Filming the birds at Chenek was both successful and entertaining. On our second day we bought a sheep and had the meat chopped up into small pieces. We kept the hind legs, liver and kidneys for ourselves, while the rest was reserved for the birds. We found a suitable site, put out some of the raw meat and then waited for something to happen. We did not have long to wait. The thick-billed and fan-tailed ravens were quickly on the spot. Both species were courageous enough to come within a few feet. They are amazing aerial acrobats and do crazy turns and somersaults in flight. The thick-billed ravens are ugly birds, black all over except for a white patch behind their heads. They have a stout and clumsy bill.

They seem mutually affectionate. I filmed one pair preening each other, carefully and thoroughly, an unusual habit in the crow family. One bird ran his beak deep among the feathers of the other, picking out parasites. He preened carefully round the back of the other's head, round the eyes, and even in the mouth which the mate obligingly opened for him. It was a touching and domestic scene and clearly part of courtship. These ravens were also very playful, often flying over to a tree and breaking off a small twig by leaning over backwards until the branch bent and finally snapped under the bird's weight. It was entertaining to watch them hanging upside down, swaying in the wind, waiting for the branch to break off.

I was sitting on a hill one day, searching through my

binoculars for any sign of a Simien fox when close by me a raven dug up an old rusty tin lid. Having perused it carefully from all angles he decided that it might be worth a chew. He grabbed the lid firmly with one claw and attempted to eat it, but obviously it did not appeal, so he dropped it disdainfully and strolled off to find something else. Another thick-billed raven appeared more intelligent than most. He wanted to receive a good scratch on the back of his head and neck, so the bird walked up to a large stone and stood in front of it with his head bowed. His mate thereupon hopped on to the stone, where it was at the right height to preen its mate's feathers. When it had soothed the standing bird in this endearing fashion, they changed places.

We got rather tired of the ravens at times because they always dived at the carefully planted meat before any other bird got a chance. Ultimately we tethered the meat to the ground so that the ravens could not fly away with it, as the main purpose of our bait was to attract the lammergeyer or bearded vulture. The lammergeyers would fly low, and close enough to give us fine opportunities to film in slow motion, but it took a great deal of time and patience before we could get them to come and settle near us on the ground. It was not until one actually landed that I realized just how big they are. They stand to a height of forty or forty-five inches with a wing span of about eight feet. Certainly a very impressive bird.

I noticed that when a lammergeyer flew off with a bone in its talons it would carefully tuck up its legs as in normal flight, thus hiding the bone from sight. This could be a means of concealing it from birds like the tawny eagle which would probably chase the lammergeyer to make it drop the bone. Many a time I saw an eagle chase some unfortunate raven which had managed to find a juicy piece of meat. Often the raven was forced to drop the meat in order to escape. It is said that lammergeyers, on finding a bone, will fly off with it up to a great height, and then drop it onto a rocky surface below in order to

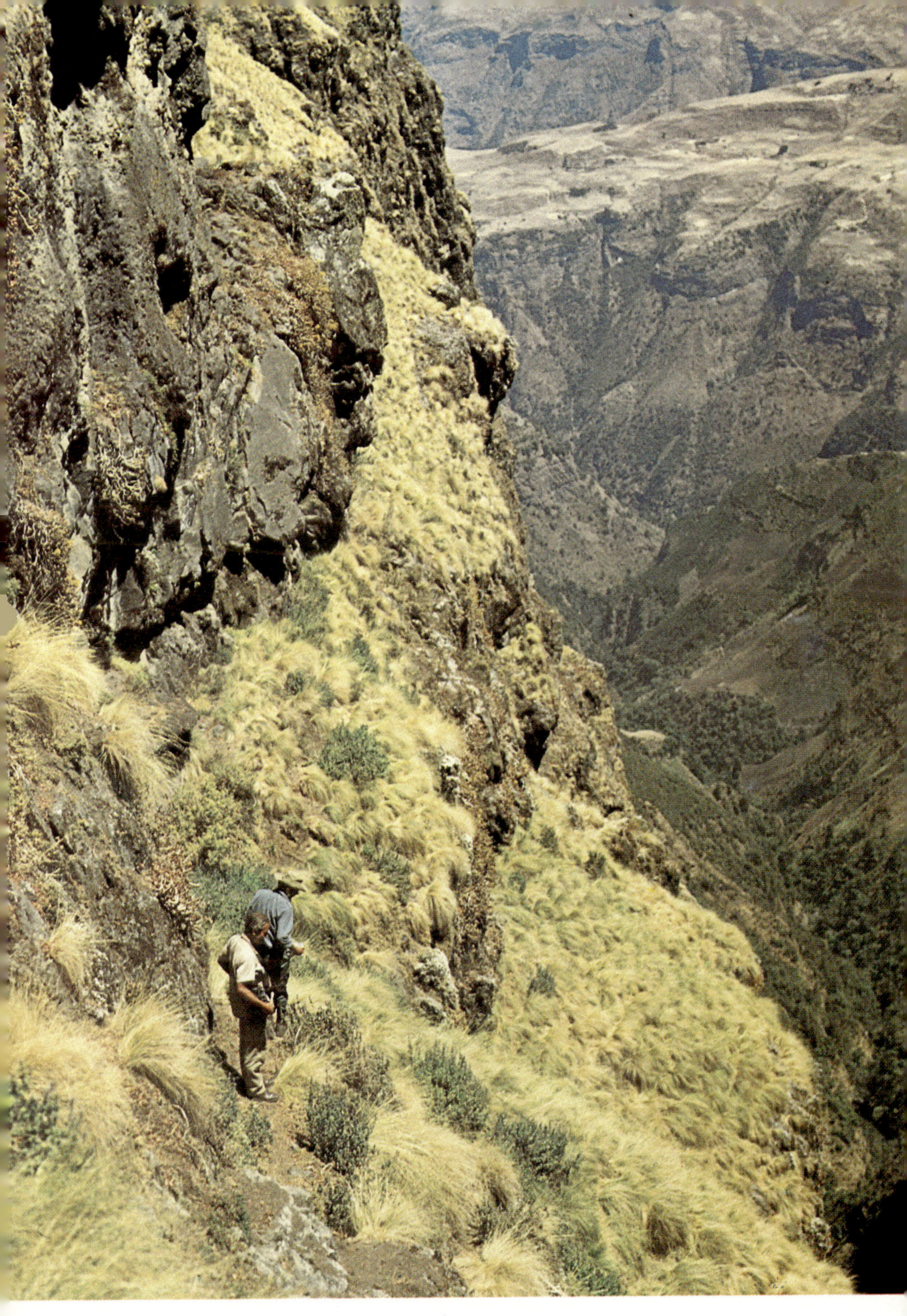

Following an ibex trail. Simien Mountains.

10,000 feet up in the Simiens.

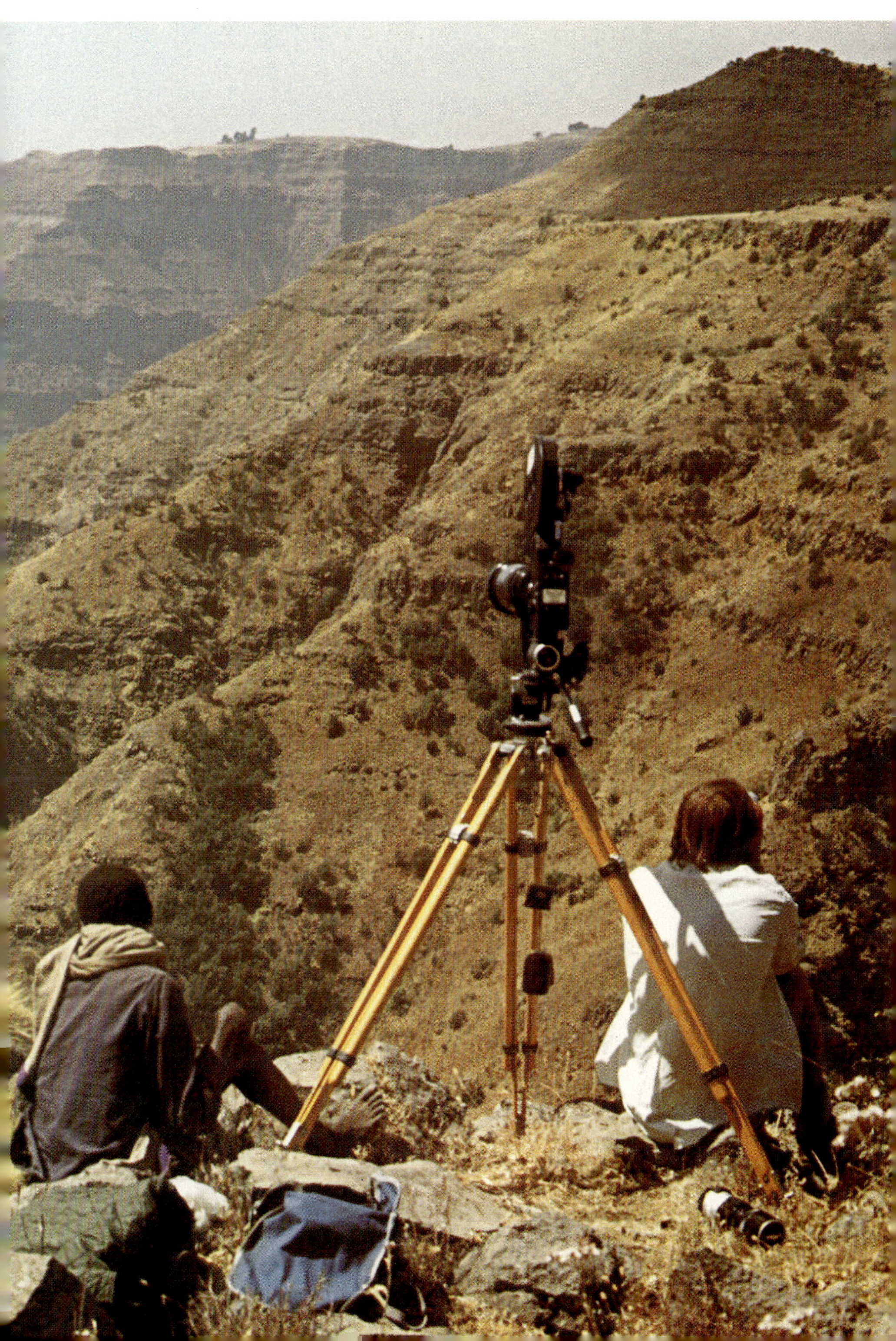

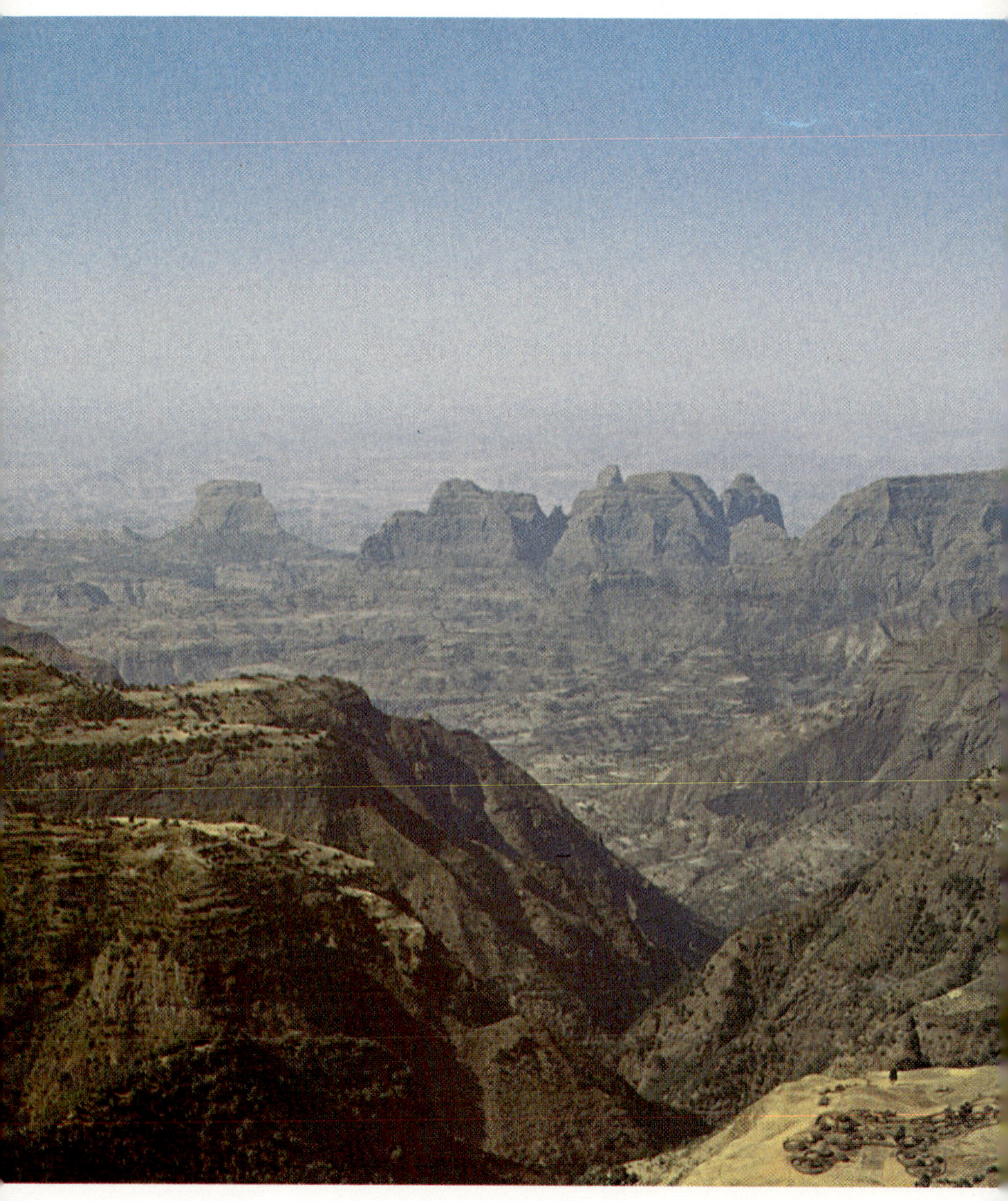

The edge of the abyss.

crack the bone open so that the bird can eat the marrow. John and I tried for days to get a bird to do this, offering juicy bones near ideal rock locations, but we never succeeded. I never met anyone who had actually witnessed this, and certainly no one has ever filmed it.

We travelled by mule from Chenek back to Geech, a journey of three hours at an altitude of 13,000 feet. Our object at Geech was to film the gelada baboons. While we were hunting for baboons we came across three klipspringers, dainty little deer, and decided to stalk them and see how close we could get. We approached stealthily from just below the edge of a cliff face, and got very near when a few baboons, watching us from the top of the cliff, started to bark. We were sure that the baboons would scare off the klipspringers, but moving a little further, more cautiously than before, we suddenly found ourselves face to face, not with klipspringers, but with a female walia ibex and her kid. They were not more than fifty feet away.

We froze. Both the ibex and her young were lying down undisturbed, so I quietly put up my tripod and very slowly fixed the camera. Once I had to remain frozen for about thirty seconds when the baboons barked, but the ibex eventually relaxed again. When the camera was fixed I very slowly edged myself up the tripod into a crouched position, eye to the camera, finger on the trigger. Still the walia female and kid lay still, although by then they seemed to be aware of my presence. We concluded afterwards that because the baboons had not run away, the ibexes presumably felt safe. Thus we secured our first footage of 'walias' as we called them.

My first close-up was of just their heads. Eventually mother and child got up and started to walk away unhurriedly feeding and turning round to regard us at intervals. Once a baby baboon bounced up to the young walia and they nosed each other. I also filmed the walias standing up on their hind legs to reach the leaves of the giant lobelia plants. Then suddenly the klipspringers came into view. The young walia joined the young klipspringers, which in turn joined up with some baboons. After a while the young walia made a mad dash for its mother who had strolled off, taking great leaps on four stiff legs. They both eventually disappeared down the face of the precipice.

Shortly after this we sighted a large troop of baboons. What we really wanted was to film them descending over the cliffs with the young playing together. We managed to get near a big troop and John and I placed ourselves so that we could film them going down the cliff face. Then we directed Lizzie Bagge, by aid of a walkie-talkie, to gently ease the baboons to the edge. The young baboons, full of curiosity, came to within twenty-five feet of us. Then all of a sudden they began to cascade down the cliffs in their hundreds. And I mean hundreds, perhaps close on five hundred baboons went down that cliff not fifty feet from us. More and more baboons kept coming over the cliff. Some slithered down at an alarming rate, others took bad routes and found themselves in a tricky position, others went down in a more leisurely fashion. There were tiny babies clutching to their mothers' backs, their tails entwined together. Bringing up the rear were the big males. The whole marvellous performance lasted for about twenty minutes by which time the light was beginning to fade.

A few days later I had another successful evening with the baboons. Hugh and I had managed to position ourselves quietly in a commanding position amid several hundred of them. We allowed them to resettle, and when we were completely surrounded by them, I started to film. I filmed the males fighting, hysterical games among the young, close-ups of their social habits as they searched each other for parasites and played in the trees. Hugh and I were engrossed for about two hours by all their activity.

Another fascinating performance that we filmed was that of the speckled pigeons. They came hurtling over the peaks to roost in the crevices below, and passed a sheer cliff face where we waited. Lizzie was posted on top of the hill to shout 'over' when she saw a group of pigeons swishing towards us like a pack of grouse. A cry from Lizzie was our cue to press the button. This way we got some good shots of the pigeons swirling up in the beautiful evening light.

We also watched the local people at work. We saw them winnowing; the men throw the corn up into the air and allow the husks to drift away in the wind. The grain then falls into one heap and the straw, being lighter than the grain but heavier than the husk, falls into another heap. They winnow the corn about three or four times to make sure that every husk and piece of straw have been separated. They sometimes have a few oxen trampling over the corn to loosen it up and make the task easier.

Then there is ploughing. Two oxen are required to pull the crude plough, which is entirely made of heavy wood except for the blade itself. To start the oxen the man controlling them whistles and gives them a hearty wallop with his whip. To stop them he taps the plough twice with a whip which, rather surprisingly, brings them to an abrupt halt. Then he lifts the whole plough up in the air while he and the oxen make a tight turn, and he starts off again. A second man walks directly behind the driver of the plough. He is armed with an instrument that looks like an adze. He uses this to break up the large hard clods of earth left by the plough.

The men plough up every inch of ground they can, not understanding the damage they are doing to the soil. This is fertile but thin as dust and once it is opened up the wind blows and the rain washes it away leaving the heavier rock that produces a poor crop. So they plough up more and more brittle areas, and so it goes on. The answer, of course, would be to move these people down the mountains to different areas, but they have lived in these summits for thousands of years and it would be impossible.

The next sequences on the shot list were to be of the walia ibex. The walia was rather slow in appearing but proved successful in the end. We were rarely able to approach nearer than five hundred yards, but with the aid of powerful lenses we managed to get some close-ups. I had constant technical problems trying to focus on infinity, but there was nothing I could do about it up in the Simiens and I had to struggle on until I could get the lens repaired in Addis. The walia is a beautiful mountain goat, much larger than a domestic goat, brown in colour although when the sun catches the coat it glints with a purple hue. Often what catches your eye first are their white knee patches, those on the front knee are the most obvious. They also have white ankles. The big males possess two very beautiful long horns which curve gracefully backwards. I saw one big male which took great delight in scratching his back by throwing his head back and using the tips of his horns. They are playful creatures. They often lower their heads and charge, then butt each other. They usually move around in small herds, the largest we saw at Chenek consisted of fourteen animals. This rare species is having a rough time in the Simiens, the only place in the world where they are found, because the animals are hunted by the Simien inhabitants both for meat and for the horns, which are used as musical instruments. A small hole is made about six inches from the top of the point, and the performer then blows down the hole. The result is not the most melodious of sounds.

At that time there were some two hundred walia ibex in the Simien National Park. Since the Park was established in 1969, the walia population had very slowly started to increase. This was largely due to efforts to control fires and woodcutting, and to preserve the natural habitat and food supply. Sadly the fires, wood-cutting and the ploughing continue outside the Park area, resulting in badly eroded land. Even now large areas in the National Park (about 60,000 acres) are completely bare of any vegetation at all. Only time will tell whether the soil will ever recover. The walia have thus been forced to the cliffs and precipices, places where man would find it difficult to follow.

We wanted to make a record of Muller and his assistant game wardens on their rounds. Muller was delighted and decided that we should go up to the top of a peak called Amba Ras and see an old walia trap used by poachers until the previous year. From a rough guess it was about five miles to the top of Amba Ras from Geech, most of it uphill. With Muller and two of his wardens, we set out at nine in the morning and reached the summit two hours later. The old walia trap was at the edge of a precipice and we followed Muller with our cameras. The path he took us along made John and me tremble at the knee. At times the width of the path narrowed to less than a foot; there was a cliff face on one side, with the occasional tuft of grass to hang on to, but on our right a sheer drop of several thousand feet, the edge of the abyss indeed! I tried to concentrate my gaze on the path and the rocks underfoot. After about half-an-hour of this dangerous and alarming experience we came finally to the old walia trap that Muller was so eager to show us.

One of Muller's men proceeded to demonstrate how the trap had worked. First he made a grass rope by pulling up large handfuls of dry grass and rubbing them between the palms of his hands. In a couple of minutes he produced six feet of very strong, tough rope. This was worked into a noose. The noose was then placed in position in a bush so that any walia passing by would have no option but to go through the noose. The noose would then tighten and the walia would die a painful death by slow strangulation. It was all too easy for the poacher.

By the end of February we packed up at Geech and argued once again with the muleteers as to how much weight each mule would carry and so began our long and dusty journey back to Addis and civilization.

In Addis I was approached by a Dr Asmaron Legesse who asked why I was not going to film the total eclipse of the sun which was due to occur on Saturday, 30 June, 1973. He said that the best place to observe the phenomenon was in Kenya on the east side of Lake Rudolph, on the route from Ethiopia to Nairobi where I was now going anyway.

The problem was that this route led through the wild desert lands which Wilfred Thesiger used to roam and which is known as 'Shifta Country' (Shifta meaning bandits from Somalia) and it was never considered safe by the establishment for unescorted travellers, least of all for unaccompanied English females.

When my intentions became known somehow in London, all hell broke loose and my father despatched a stream of cables insisting that under no circumstances was I even to contemplate such a trip. He even quoted a number of distinguished Ethiopian and other authorities to dissuade me.

I have to admit that I was at first disconcerted by all this finger wagging from afar, for it was perfectly true that five years earlier just after my father had camped with Prince Philip on the south-east shores of Lake Rudolph, the place had been stormed in the night and a party which included an Italian priest had been murdered. However, having weighed up all the pros and cons, and having found out that Hugh Smith would keep me company, I decided to provoke no more cables or hysteria, but simply set off in the night and crossed the hundreds of miles of exciting moonscape past Lake Rudolph to Nairobi.

FOUR

Journey into Darkness

Hugh Smith, who was teaching at a university in Addis, but whose students were on strike, helped me pack up the vehicle and trailer with equipment and by the time we had finished I do not think a matchbox could have been fitted in. We were so late when we had finished that I intended to drive to Marsabit, near Lake Rudolph, where we were to meet Dr Legesse, without stopping. If some Shifta loomed up I would simply put my foot down and run them over.

We left Addis shortly after midday and I drove for the first twelve hours whilst Hugh dozed off occasionally in the passenger seat. The tarmac road ended at Shashamane, two hundred and fifty kilometres to the south of Addis and from then on the roads were badly corrugated, wet and very muddy. At about one o'clock the following morning we struggled into a little village called Dilla. It was in total darkness and I got out to stretch my legs and hand over the wheel to Hugh. After a cigarette we drove on.

I was exhausted and soon dropped off into a state of semi-consciousness, but it was not to last for long.

At a fork in the track ahead, Hugh decided to turn left, but soon the track started to turn north by the compass in the car, whereas we were meant to be heading south. So back we went to the fork and took the turning to the right.

After about half an hour we came to a steep climb, but what with the immense load in the car, the pouring rain and slippery mud, we could not get up. So again we turned round and went back past the fork, until we found a camp just off the road. It had been set up by workers rebuilding the road, and after a while we found a guard at the main entrance. It was then five o'clock in the morning, bitterly cold and still pouring with rain.

The guard was helpful and told us that the two roads we had been on were both wrong for going south. There was in fact a third road, which we had missed altogether. He drew us a map on the ground, and we thanked him, gave him some cigarettes and set off once more. Although it was still dark we found the missing road and I tried again to settle down to sleep whilst Hugh battled on through the mud. As dawn broke, clouds were swirling around the car, it was still horribly cold and I pulled the blanket tight around me before dozing off again.

I woke up as we passed through a ramshackle village called Agere Mariam and just after it a new surface began. At last Hugh was able to increase speed. We came round a corner and directly in front of us was an expanse of dark red, wet, very slippery mud. We hit it at 40 m.p.h. and immediately the car began to slide gracefully about. Hugh struggled to keep it under control, but we did a U-turn and went off the road backwards crashing down a ten foot embankment into a ditch and landing on our side.

I opened my eyes and found Hugh on top of me still holding the steering wheel. I asked him kindly to switch off the ignition and open his door. I could already hear excited voices outside and saw several surprised faces when Hugh and I eventually managed to emerge. Many eager hands were outstretched to help us.

I looked at the car and groaned while Hugh had gone white and his hands were shaking. I counted about thirty Ethiopians around the car and asked them if they would help us to lift it back on to its wheels. We all tried several times, but could not get the car to budge, so I had to take all the equipment off the roof and we tried again. This time with much heaving and puffing we slowly got it back on to its wheels. But of course it was still at the bottom of the deep ditch.

I went round to check the damage. The right back wing was buckled and almost torn off, the left front wing was badly damaged, and acid from the battery was leaking onto the accelerator spring. (This meant that from then on I had to use my toe to flick the pedal up to reduce speed. I had a very sore toe by the time I got to Nairobi.) The roof rack was bent, but worst of all, all the bolts securing the top half of the body to the bottom had snapped. Any hope of getting to Marsabit that night was now out of the question.

One of the locals then ran back to the road-builders' camp for help and after an hour a Land-Rover and a bulldozer arrived to drag my poor motor car out of the ditch. All the equipment that I had taken off my roof-rack was loaded into the Land-Rover and we were towed back to camp.

The manager examined my battered vehicle and finally called for one of his mechanics. The roof-rack was beaten back into shape and the two wings forced away from the tyres. But it was the top half of the body that I was most worried about. A lorry with a winch on it was backed up to my Land-Rover, and with huge tractor tyres placed between it and the lorry, an immense rope was passed round the body of the Land-Rover. When some old bolts, found in the back of the workshop, had been driven into the holes to secure the top half to the bottom half of my Land-Rover, the winch was slowly turned, the rope tightened, and the roof began to groan and squeak as the metal was pulled very roughly back into shape.

The vehicle still looked awful but once I was able to close the back door again, I thought we could probably continue on our way. So I thanked everyone, packed up all the equipment and with much waving we continued on our way.

Hugh and I were so tired, hungry and miserable that we

decided to stop off at another ramshackle place called Yabello for the night. But first Yabello had no hot water or a bath; secondly the only food we could find were some eggs; thirdly we were each given a bed with no sheets; and finally the whole village stank abominably and dogs barked all night long. At six the next morning we therefore dug the manager of the so-called hotel out of his bed, paid our bill and set off for the border.

From Yabello the road began to deteriorate still further and at times vanished altogether, so that we had to take a guess as to where the track should go. We got lost, the Land-Rover broke down, and we spent another night on the road. The last stretch to Moyale, on the border, a distance of about seventy miles, took us over six hours on the worst roads in the world. By five in the evening we arrived at the border post of Moyale and presented ourselves to the Kenyan Immigration and Customs Post.

For once all went well and within an hour we were on our way again. The Kenyan road seemed like a motorway. For the first time in days we were able to move with reasonable comfort and we drove non-stop. Most of the journey was in darkness, but even so we saw a few animals in the lights, giraffe, hyenas, gazelles and white-tailed mongooses. The giraffes were tall and graceful, we passed one six feet away and it appeared quite undisturbed. We reached Marsabit at one in the morning.

The manager of the camp organized a meal, and hot water for a shower which was wonderful. We certainly slept well that night, until a boy woke me the next morning at seven with fresh tea.

No one was sure where the party from Ethiopia might be so we decided to drive into Marsabit to see if we could find anyone. In the main street of the town I noticed an African frantically waving at me, and on stopping I found to my delight Dr Legesse himself running towards us. I explained why we were so late, and he took us to his camp in the forest near Marsabit. Hundreds of people from America and Europe were pouring into the area for the total eclipse, so I was very glad that I was in a quiet little village and not out with the milling mass elsewhere.

Dr Legesse's camp was cosy and well set up. It was the main 'eclipse headquarters', with several smaller camps in various villages round it. Dr Legesse wanted me to go to a little Samburu village looking out over the Chalbi Desert. We went along together and found five other people there. Each had a specific job to do during the eclipse, sound recording, photographing, filming, making notes, and so on.

Apart from filming the eclipse itself, we also wanted to film the inhabitants of the Samburu village, during the event. We therefore went to see the wells where the Samburu cattle are watered and drinking water is collected by the women. The wells are up to thirty feet deep, with water troughs made out of clay for the cattle at the top. About every four or five feet down there is a small platform big enough for a man to stand. It takes six or seven to get the water out of the well into the troughs at the top. One man stands in the water scooping the water into buckets. The second man stands or sits on the platform above, and another sits above him, and so on, until the buckets reach the top chap, who fills the troughs. The buckets are made of goat's skin, and several are used at a time so that there is a steady stream of full buckets going up and empty ones going down. To keep the rhythm, which is important, all the men sing lustily and one is tempted to join in.

The night before the eclipse we were all called back to Dr Legesse's main camp for a final briefing. Special fast film was handed out, cameras and lenses cleaned and polished, and arrangements made for the camels to transport all our gear next morning.

On the morning of the eclipse the view from our village across the Chalbi Desert was lovely; ahead of us lay the mountains in the distance, and behind them stretched Lake Rudolph, the jade sea.

As I waited for the eclipse to start I went around the village filming what I could of the people at work or play. None of them much liked my camera, but the children were not too difficult until their mothers whisked them away. I filmed a tiny child playing in the dust and stones, the huts, the main 'street', the enclosures in which the camels, cattle and goats were kept at night. A thick wall of thorn bushes piled high on top of each other was their only defence against wild animals.

The eclipse was due to start on Saturday at three in the afternoon, although this was not at first apparent. Then I began to watch the slow progress of the eclipse through a layer of processed negative film. Without highly specialized filters one cannot film the partial eclipse. Only during its totality can one finally point a camera directly at the sun with no harm to the eyes.

About an hour after a sandwich lunch, I began to notice the first sign of fading light. The impression was of a very heavy rainstorm approaching, a strange yellowish light burnt out all the blues. I saw the cattle from the village being urged across the plain, herded into their enclosure and barricaded in as though for the night. Then the villagers started to take refuge in their huts, closing the doors. They had been warned by the Government to go indoors during the eclipse and to stay there until it was over. They had no idea what an eclipse was or what was going to happen, but as the light failed their courage failed them too. The women picked up their children and ran home. Soft moaning sounds, praying and singing, could be heard from the settlement.

The village then became absolutely quiet. Cattle, camels, and goats, all in their pens, lay down as if it was night, even the dogs stopped barking. Bird song ceased and silence descended on the whole area. The light grew more mysterious by the second, yellower and yellower as the other colours faded out.

The total eclipse was due at exactly thirty seconds before four o'clock. Five and a half minutes before, the light decreased markedly and ninety seconds to zero darkness accelerated, like lights being dimmed in a cinema. For about fifteen seconds before, and after the total eclipse had occurred, wonderful and weird shadow bars ran quivering across the ground. By then it was impossible for the camera to record anything. The shadow bars were thought to be some kind of reflection from the sun.

Total eclipse lasted four minutes and nineteen seconds. During that time it was as night with a moon shining. Along the horizon was a sunset glow, and against it objects could be seen in silhouette. The stars confirmed that they are always in the sky during the day. I filmed the silhouettes of the mud huts with the eclipse overhead.

I moved quickly into one of the enclosures and filmed the cattle in silhouette while they were lying down. There was not a movement, nor a sound except for the wind in the scattered palms. It was an experience I shall never forget. The temperature had dropped considerably when most of the sun had gone, and it did not warm up until part of it reappeared. As I reached the end of the village I came out into open hillside and panned slowly with my camera from the horizon to the still eclipsed sun. Then I started back again through the village. It was well timed because just as I began to film the apparently deserted place, the eclipse ended. First came the amazing shadow bars again followed by a rush of light. The village emerged from darkness and I was ready to record the community's return to life.

It was ten or fifteen minutes before the light was normal. The people waited for a further ten minutes before slowly they began to come out. They looked around and blinked in the strong sunlight, and then the men went about the task of herding their cattle out of the pens and taking them to the plain to feed. Then the dogs got up and began to bark and sniff around, the children went back to playing and the women resumed their daily work.

I filmed what I could of the people back at work. A young girl was soon pounding grain outside her hut, another girl having her hair plaited by an old woman, another old woman weaving her basket sitting beside her hut in the sun.

I found out much later that all the tribes and people who lived in the direct path of the eclipse and had seen what had happened, had decided that only the 'white man' had the powers to make the sun go out. They were all full of wonder and amazement, quite convinced that it had somehow been decreed and arranged.

That night I slept in the village in my sleeping bag, on the hard uneven ground and woke up to find my ears full of dust. I organized a camel to carry my equipment to Dr Legesse's camp. Back there people were slowly turning up with all the film, photographs and recordings taken during the eclipse. I gave Dr Legesse my film to support his coverage and then began to pack up my Land-Rover once more. All I wanted to do now was to get on to Nairobi, though I was acutely aware that I had been immensely privileged to experience a notable wonder of the universe, in a part of our planet that has hardly changed over millions of years. The awful slog from Ethiopia had won a dramatic sequel.

FIVE

Life in a Swamp

The idea for my next film expedition was born when I was still in Ethiopia. While I was marooned in a village there called Gambala, waiting for a flooded river to subside, I set eyes on a most extraordinary bird. I really thought I was seeing things at first, so I wiped my binoculars and took another look. But it was still there and from that moment I decided I would make a film about the oddest looking bird in the world – one which I later discovered was called the whale-headed stork or shoebill.

Several months later in August 1973, I flew over to Frankfurt Zoo and was taken round by our friend Bernard Grzimek. I saw, at close range, their five shoebills and for a whole day I talked to the men who looked after them. I made notes about their feeding habits, where they were to be found, breeding times and so on.

To film shoebills in the wild I had apparently a choice of three countries; Uganda, which I ruled out as I had no intention of making friends with Idi Amin; Sudan, and Zambia. The Southern Sudd in Sudan looked good but once I had done some research on Sudan itself, I changed my mind. A civil war had just finished there and the country did not look too inviting for a lone female. Roads and bridges had been blown up, hardly any petrol was available, and a host of other problems presented themselves. I therefore turned to Zambia, and the Bangweulu Swamps.

So, for the fourth time, I went out to Africa and flew to

Lusaka with a letter of introduction to the Director of the National Parks, John Clarke, who advised me to make a reconnaissance. He was enthusiastic about the film and drove me five hundred miles north from Lusaka. He told me a lot about wildlife in Zambia and it appeared that no commercial films had yet been made in the country, and certainly not in the swamps. When we reached the edge of the swamps and John's Fiat could go no further, we found the resident biologist, Ian Manning, waiting for us. A South African by birth, he had already been living in the swamps for two years and so was able to give me much valuable advice.

After a short rest, John returned to Lusaka, while Ian and I climbed into his battered old Land-Rover and rattled over rough ground till we reached a little village, Ngungwa, beyond which no vehicle could go. Here we loaded up a canoe with an outboard engine and chugged or punted our way through little canals in the swamps for two hours until we finally landed on a small island called Chikuni. By then we were in darkness.

I saw my first shoebill in flight during that two hour journey through David Livingstone's country, just as the light was falling. This was an unforgettable experience. Livingstone died only thirty miles from the island of Chikuni and I am sure that what I saw that evening was exactly what Livingstone had seen a hundred years before. We punted our way in and out of the papyrus and along little cleared rivers until we got to within a mile of Chikuni Island.

Here we finally had to abandon the canoe and wade waist deep, carrying everything on our heads, because the equatic vegetation was too thick for the canoe. We squelched our way to the island and arrived at the Mannings' little prefabricated house. I was filthy, soaked to the skin, frozen stiff and very tired. After a hot bath and a good dinner, I collapsed on their living-room sofa for the night.

Chikuni was 1000 yards long by 200 yards wide, with a

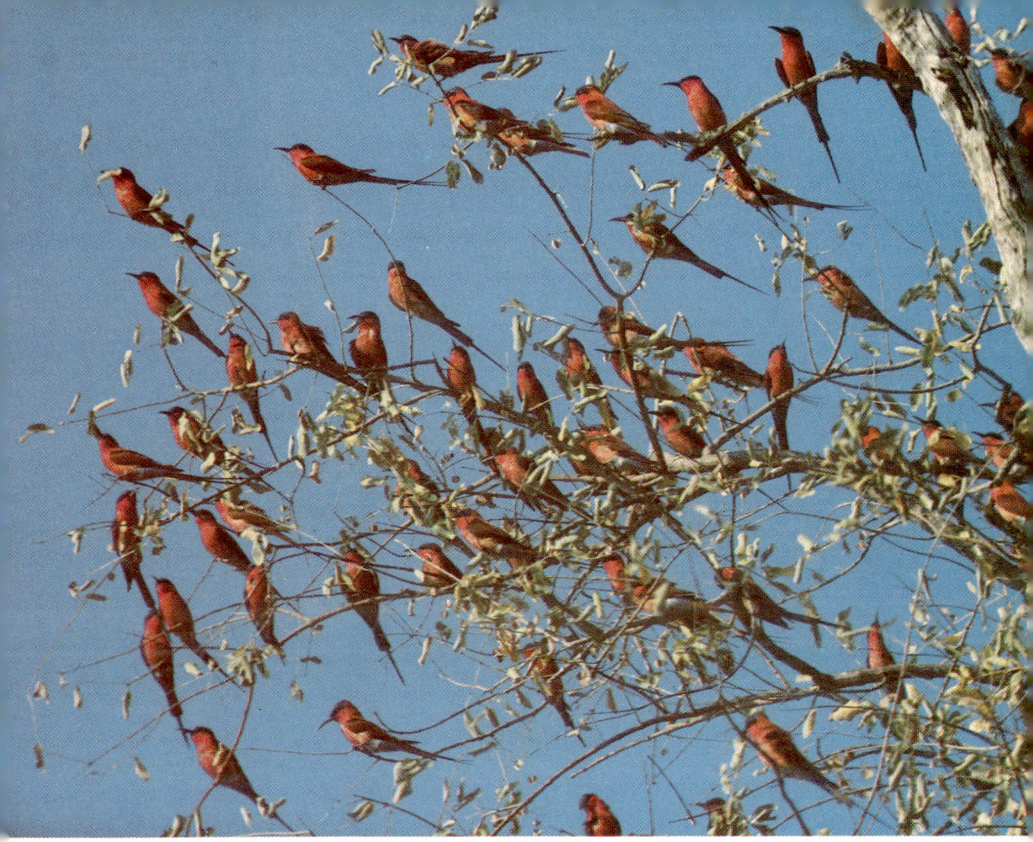

Carmine bee-eaters above their cliff.

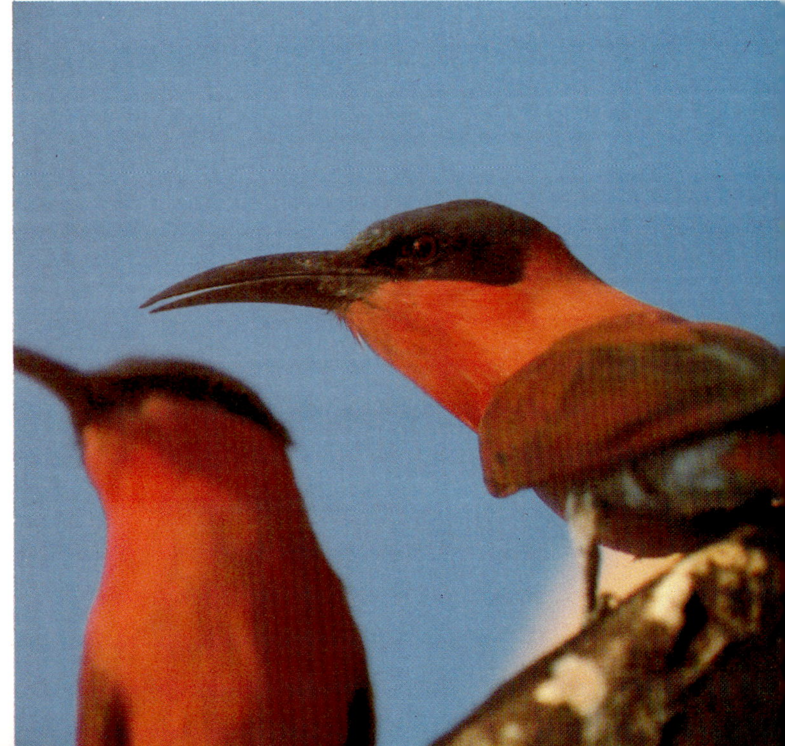

Carmines, the most beautiful bee-eaters.

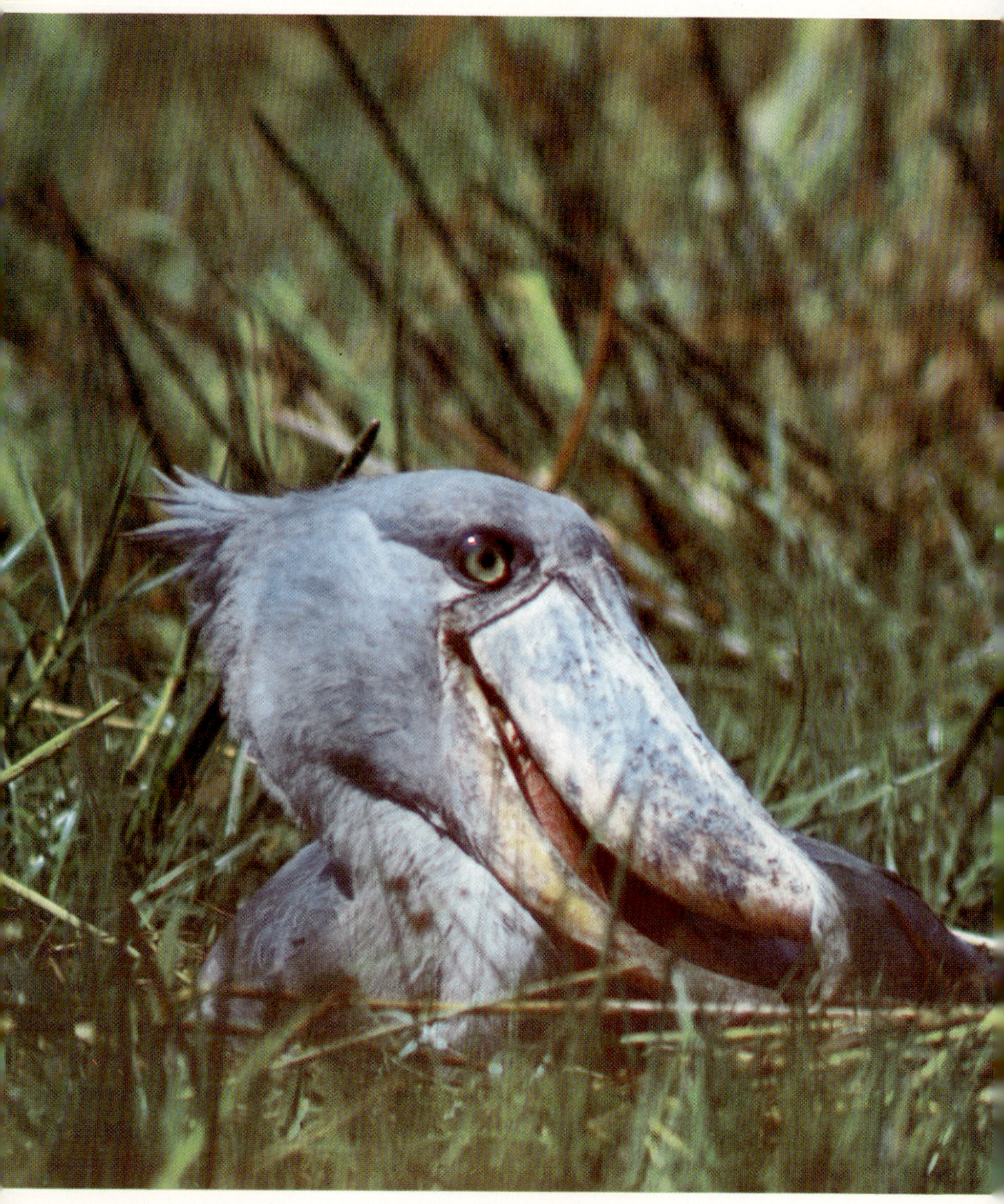

My shoebill mother.

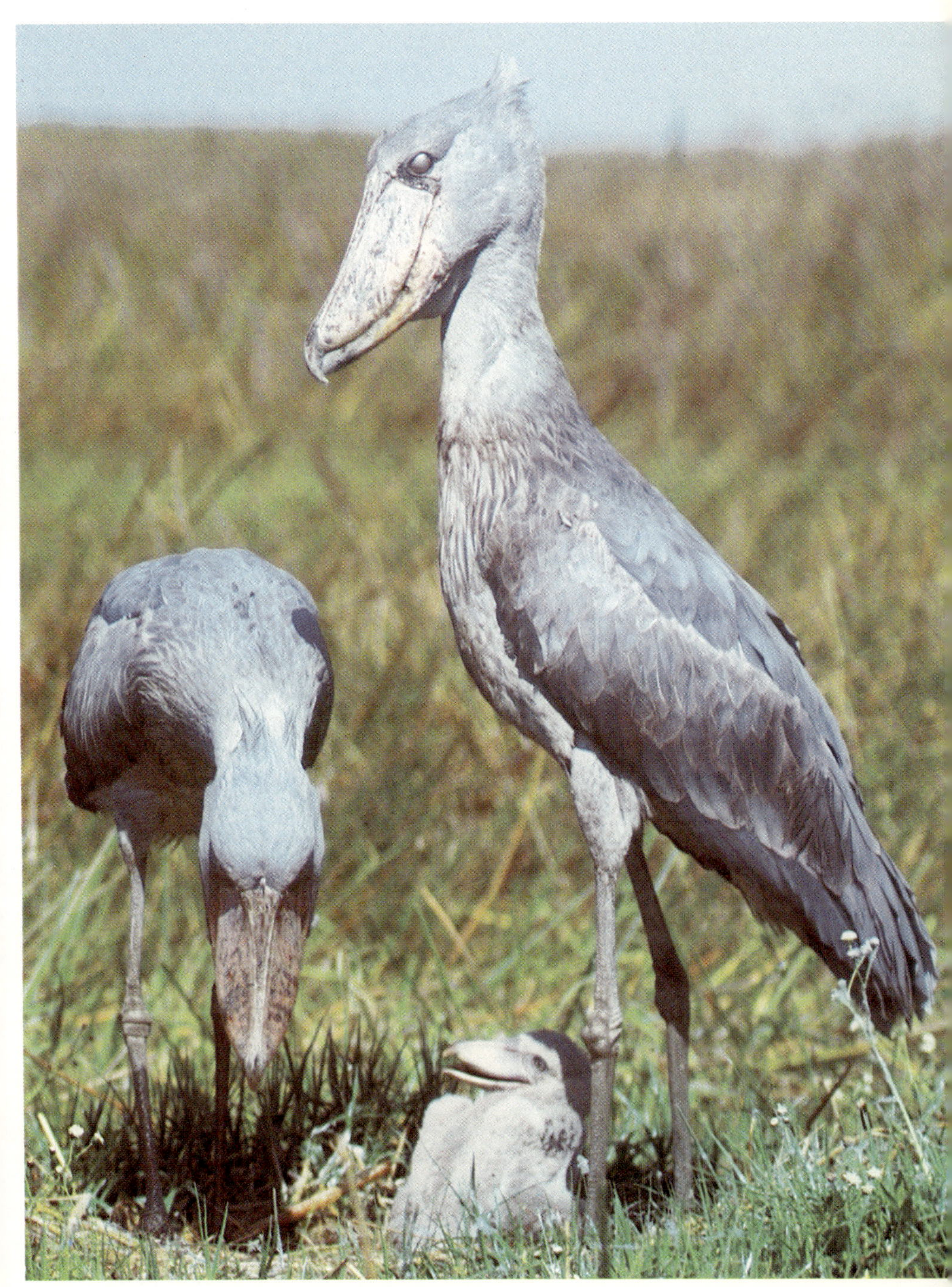

Shoebills at their nest.

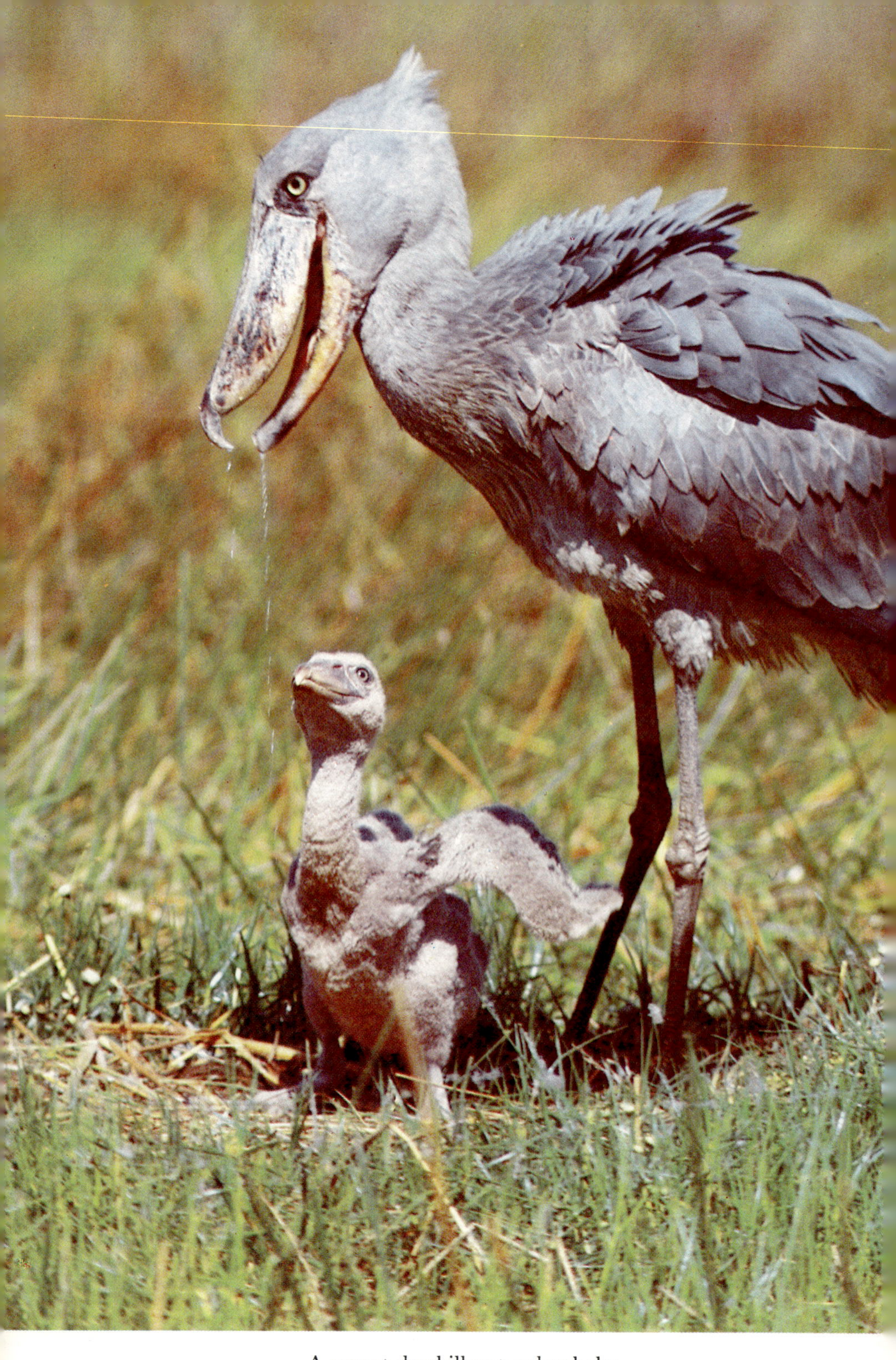

A parent shoebill waters her baby.

grass airstrip running through the centre. On one side was the prefab, a store house and a guest hut which was later to be my home for nearly a year. On the other side of the strip were some tin huts where a couple of game guards and a few house servants lived.

I only had one full day with Ian in the swamps to have a first look round for the shoebills. Punting in a canoe we saw a total of eight shoebills and actually managed to find a nest with one egg in it, which thrilled me. Ian told me that he had made a hide on one of the canoes so that he could take photographs of the birds on the nest, but he had found that they were very timid and easily upset. Going round by canoe was hard work, even when we were punting in clear water, and at intervals we had to get out and push through thick papyrus beds. The swamps not only revealed all the water birds in the book but a wide variety of animals, lions, elephants, black lechwe, sitatunga and many other animals. On that first day I realized just how much there was in the swamps to film.

In the evening I talked with the Mannings, making notes about the best times and places for filming the different birds and animals. The following day, having got the information I needed, a light aircraft picked me up from the grass strip and flew me back to Lusaka.

My next visit to the swamps was six months later, with my father and Peter and Philippa Scott. The first thing I noticed was how dry Chikuni was compared to my last visit. The island was now brown and the swamps had receded about a mile from the house, whereas before it had been only a hundred yards away.

We spent two nights in the swamps. We were able to go out in Ian's Land-Rover over the dry areas to look at herds of black lechwe found only in the Bangweulu. I had seen Kafue lechwe which are much like them, but these males had black shoulders and front legs. The Game Department airboat was also operating, so that we were able to go out even further into the swamps and cover wide areas in a reasonable time. These are splendid machines, constructed especially for swamps. They have a fibre-glass flat-bottomed hull with a Lycoming 180 aircraft engine on the back and a wooden propeller. Their main disadvantage is the appalling noise.

We found three shoebills during our stay, not as many as I had seen during my previous visit, but they were the first my father and the Scotts had seen in the wild. We revelled in the swamps, with all the water birds living just outside our hut, and spent our happiest hours in the canoes, creeping round the papyrus beds and through the reeds, as closely as possible to every form of life we could find.

After this second visit I decided that the shoebill film should definitely go ahead, and wrote out a long report with my ideas for the film, which *Survival* in London finally accepted. Then came the forbidding task of transporting all my equipment down through Tanzania and Zambia into the swamps.

Since 1972 I had been employing the young African Ndungu from Naivasha. He had worked with me at Naivasha and begged me to take him to Zambia. First I had to get him a passport; then I arranged for him to have driving lessons. He failed his test the first time but managed to pass the second. Finally we packed everything into my car just after Christmas and at the beginning of 1975 we set off for the swamps.

After many canoe journeys with all my equipment and food stores for several months, I was finally installed on Chikuni Island, which was still dry but did not remain so for long. The hardboard hut that had been lent to me by the Zambia Game Department had been used as a store house. Ian and Cathy Manning had cleared it out but it was very dirty, with broken windows, holes in the rotten walls, no shelves or tables, and only cold water. For the first week I converted it into my home for the next ten months. Ian found some plywood and I set to work building shelves, tables, and mending the worst holes in the walls. Once my gas cylinders had arrived by canoe, I got the refrigerator going and tackled the cooker, but without spectacular success.

Neither of the airboats were working when I arrived. Ian finally got his going, but I had to make do with a canoe for the first two months until I had arranged for a mechanic to come up from Lusaka, five hundred miles away, to give it a major overhaul.

Ndungu and I went out in the canoe as much as possible, punting ourselves through the dense papyrus. It was slow, hard, hot work and sometimes we had to wade through dense vegetation pushing the canoe ahead of us, soaked from the waist down. But it was quiet and peaceful and ideal for stalking wildlife.

We decided to build reed hides in various locations to film the lechwe, sitatunga, birds and anything else that came along. Unknowingly I built one hide right on top of an ants' nest. It was not until I looked down and saw hundreds of black ants crawling up my legs that I realized what I had done. I jumped into the water and sat down up to my neck. I sent Ndungu back to camp in the canoe to get some petrol to soak the area of the hide and get rid of the ants. I built seven hides in all and after leaving them for a while for the animals to get used to them, I ultimately sat in them for up to ten hours a day.

The weather during January and February was frightful. At one time it rained solidly for ten days and nights without a break, and forced me to stay indoors. I checked my cameras over and over again, wrote up my notes and read nearly a book a day. How relieved I was when it finally stopped and the sun struggled out once again. As soon as the rains had eased off, Ian started to catch sitatunga for his research project and I went out with him every day for a week to help the operation. Ian would chase the sitatunga in his airboat. Catching the females was no problem, sometimes very funny. Ian's helpers were posted in the bow of the airboat, crouched down and ready to jump on top of an animal as the airboat caught up with it. Quite often a helper would time his jump badly and miss the animal, landing with a huge splash in the swamp. All the females and young sitatunga were captured this way. No harm came to either humans or animals in two feet of water.

Catching the adult males was another matter. They have long, sharp horns. It was too dangerous to jump on them in case the jumper got stabbed. They are strong and it would be difficult for one man to hold one down, so we used long bamboo poles with a noose on the end. As the airboat caught up with the animal, the noose would be placed over the horns and then the airboat was slowed down. The end of the rope was tied to the airboat and the animal was brought to a halt. The helpers would then jump out and run over to the sitatunga, tie it up and carry it back to the boat.

The boat could only carry about six sitatunga at a time. Ian injected them with a tranquillizer to calm them down, their feet were tied and they were blindfolded. They were then taken to a dry island where a camp had been set up. The animal would then be weighed, measured, blood samples taken, tooth impressions recorded, ticks removed and bottled, and finally collared with a number. It was then untied and released, still a little shaken from its two hour ordeal.

Once I had finished filming the capture, I helped Ian in any way I could, and even went so far as to 'jump' six sitatunga myself. Although sitatunga are rarely seen and therefore considered scarce, Ian estimated that Bangweulu holds about fifteen thousand. They inhabit the wet, dense, high vegetation and have to be flushed out to be seen at all.

In the evenings, when I had nobody to talk to, I suffered from loneliness, but I managed to get through a great deal of work. I filmed the black lechwe, and just about all the wildlife in the swamps, buffalo, elephants and two lions, which I stalked on foot for an hour with Ian, who was thankfully armed with a rifle. These were a male and a female, calmly walking through an open part of the swamp. Ian grabbed his .270, and I my Arriflex, and we jumped off the airboat, leaving Cathy behind to watch out for us. I had never stalked a wild lion before, so I stayed behind Ian peering nervously over his shoulder. Some of the time we were up to our waists in water with rifle and camera held high. What on earth am I doing, I thought, wading up to my waist in water, tracking two possibly ferocious lions just for ten seconds of film? Why wasn't I back at home playing tennis or watching telly?

We kept the male lion in sight and followed him, but soon lost sight of the female. The female is the more dangerous, she is the one that hunts and makes the kill. I felt certain that while Ian and I were stalking the male, the female was stalking us. For at least an hour we struggled forward, stopping every twenty yards or so to peer through binoculars to see if we could spot him. We knew roughly where he ought to be, but he had obviously stopped and hidden, and was no doubt watching our approach.

Ian stood on top of an anthill and listened. Nothing. We jumped on top of another anthill, and while we were practically in mid-air, the lion roared not twenty feet away. Up came rifle and camera at the same instant. The lion, a beautiful specimen, jumped from his hiding place, a large anthill in a thick bush, and dashed off through the swamps. I could feel Ian fingering the trigger but he contained himself and lowered the rifle. All I got were a few feet of film of the lion bounding away over the anthills, but it was good enough to include in the final shoebill film.

After a few weeks I started to notice an increase in the number of shoebills, and saw thirteen at one time standing on a flooded plain. I stalked them all day in the canoe, without much success. However, it was fairly obvious that their breeding season was nearing, as I saw several birds chasing each other in the air and making a clapping noise with their beaks. This was in March.

There were times during those ten long months in the swamps when I craved for company. The Mannings had to spend more and more time away in Lusaka, leaving me entirely alone. During the day when I was out filming I was happy to be by myself, but sometimes in the evenings, particularly, I longed to talk to someone about the film, or the birds and animals, or really about anything at all. I think my sanity was saved by a great white pelican called Fred.

Fred was handed over to the Mannings shortly before I arrived at Chikuni by a local. The man who brought him in said that the parents had deserted the young chick. The young pelican was then cared for by Ian and Cathy and was fed on fish caught in the swamps. Fred became tame very quickly and enjoyed human company. It did not take long for Fred and myself to develop a great affection and respect for each other.

During the day when I was out filming, Fred would sit by the door of my house waiting for me to come home. On seeing me return, he would waddle up with much honking, wings outstretched, finally lowering his head in a submissive gesture. If I was not away he would stay close by my side in the house, leaving his mark everywhere, or he would follow close behind me outside. He was very possessive, and hated anyone to come too close to me. For instance if anyone wanted to shake my hand, he would launch himself at the unfortunate stranger, grabbing an arm or leg in his beak, which could cause nasty scratches. He liked me to sit on the ground so that he could preen my long hair. Sometimes he got a bit rough about it, and ended up nipping my ears or my neck.

But one day Fred abruptly left me. I was sad to see him go, but also delighted that he had decided on the great adventure of returning to the wild. For some time I had noticed that he was getting itchy feet, or itchy wings. He used to stand on one of my empty fuel drums, facing the wind, and flap his wings. I would run down the airstrip to encourage him to fly. It was not long before he was soaring aloft. At first he would circle round the island several times and then land right at my feet, obviously pleased with himself. And then one day Fred found himself a lady pelican, and understandably enough that was the end of our beautiful friendship.

For human company my friend Jenny Slater came out to stay from Kenya and we had many adventures together. On one occasion we were in the airboat looking for shoebills. Finally we found one, and turned off the engine and sat back to watch. After a while the bird took flight and landed about a mile away, so I switched on the engine to follow. Nothing happened.

I spent the next hour dismantling the starter which I knew was the cause of the trouble, but I just could not find the fault. As it was late I decided in the end that we must wade back to Chikuni, about three miles away. With my .458 rifle on my shoulder we set off. It was the longest three miles under the scorching sun that I have ever undertaken. Most of the time we walked in water up to our thighs, sometimes up to our waists. We were sure that every clump of reeds had a lion hiding in it or that crocodiles were watching our every movement. Then suddenly, without any warning, we both sank into a bog up to our necks. As we sank we clutched at each other and prayed. Our prayer was answered because we both hit the bottom and stopped only neck deep in water and mud.

In May I started to fly over the swamps with some friends in Zambia, Ian and Rose McLeod, who had their own aircraft. For three days we searched for shoebill nests within a ten mile radius. I found three nests from the air, but having located them from above, I then had to find them from swamp level. The nearest was only fifteen minutes in the airboat and it contained two white, chalky eggs. I had no idea when the eggs had been laid, so could not judge when they would hatch. The two other nests were miles from the house and took an hour and a half to reach by the airboat, which made them impractical to visit every day. Each contained one egg.

At this stage I left the shoebills for a few days, as I wanted to film a new activity which was starting at Chikuni. President Kaunda had asked for one hundred black lechwe to be taken from Bangweulu and reinstated at a place called Chinsali. Chinsali was where Kenneth Kaunda grew up as a boy, and he could remember seeing them as a child, but due to poaching the lechwe had either been killed or deserted and none had been seen there for some time. He had ordered the Air Force to handle the transportation. In the middle of May the aircraft landed on the small grass strip at Chikuni to start the exercise. We had at our disposal a Caribou, which carried thirty lechwe at a time, and a Beaver in support. The Zambian pilots were very friendly and helpful and I was impressed at the way they handled the huge Caribou in such a confined space.

Once the Air Force arrived, Ian started catching lechwe. It took three days hard work in the airboat, hour upon hour. Catching lechwe was much the same as catching male sitatunga. A pole and noose were used and slipped over the horns or head, and the animal was brought gently to a halt without any injury being done. The animal was then blindfolded and tranquillized and carried to the airboat.

When Ian had half a dozen lechwe he took them back to camp where they were laid under large tarpaulins to shelter them from the sun. It would take Ian until about two in the afternoon each day to collect a full load of thirty lechwe. They were then carefully loaded into the Caribou and flown to Chinsali, which took about another hour. From there they travelled in lorries for a further hour into the swampland where they were released.

Now it was time to concentrate again on my shoebill film, so I went to have another look at the nearest nest with the two eggs in it. They had still not hatched, and I began a patient vigil.

SIX

Almost a Dodo?

It took me almost a month to persuade the nesting shoebills to accept me. Each day I would push my canoe nearer, making as little noise and movement as possible. On top of the canoe I had built a hide of dry reeds and grass with windows through which to film.

After the first month the female shoebill, who was the most tolerant, took off from her nest, flew round my canoe and landed not twenty feet away directly behind me, so that she could see straight into the back of the hide. She was obviously a very curious bird, and just wanted to know what I was up to. From that day on I took down my hide and filmed in full view of the birds. It did not appear to bother them in the least.

At the beginning I had trouble with the noise of the camera motor. It upset the shoebills and made them jump every time I switched on. I padded the camera very heavily at first and then slowly allowed the noise to increase until they failed to notice it any longer. Every day I set out in the airboat and travelled for ten to fifteen minutes to within two hundred yards of the nest. From there I unloaded my cameras into the canoe and set them up. Then I had to push hard in water up to my waist through very thick reeds to within thirty feet of the nest. Quietly I would climb aboard the canoe and there I stayed for the next nine hours watching and waiting, always at the ready.

The nest was built on a floating island of vegetation. It did not actually move, but was thick enough to stand the weight of the shoebills, but not of myself. It was made of long dried grasses and was about three feet across, with a slight depression in the middle. More grass was continually added to the nest throughout the time the birds lived there, otherwise it would probably have sunk.

During the incubation period there was very little activity. I concentrated on getting close-ups, showing in detail the beak, eyes and the absurd little tuft of feathers on the top of their heads, the wing feathers, legs and their enormous feet. If it was cloudy or a cool day the sitting bird would not move for hours on end, only getting up occasionally to stretch its legs, ruffle its feathers, or have a drink and preen.

But if it was a hot sweltering day, then the birds were kept busy cooling the eggs. The parent would get up off the nest, wade about six feet to where the long grass was not so thick, and scoop up a beakful of water, tipping the head back to hold the water at the back of its gullet. It would then hurry back to the eggs, and standing over them, lower its head, open its beak slightly and dribble the water over the eggs. Having splashed the eggs, the bird would often go and pull up a mouthful of wet grass and pad this around the eggs as well.

Rolling and turning the eggs would then follow, using either feet or beak, and much re-arranging of the nesting material. Finally the bird would slowly lower itself back on to the eggs, shuffling and wriggling to get comfortable. But often it was not as comfortable as it would like so the bird would stand up once again, adjust a few stems of grass and try once more. One day the female had a real problem with a few stems of grass, and sat down and stood up seven times, before finally wriggling well down on to the eggs and dozing off.

When the shoebills met during the day to change over at the nest the bird arriving would land about fifty feet from the nest and walk the rest of the way. Once the two adults were together they raised their heads and clapped their beaks, the male uttering a strange hissing noise at the conclusion of the clapping. Then they lowered their heads and swayed them from side to side, perhaps with an occasional clap. This completed the greeting display.

At other times there appeared to be little love between the two birds and as soon as the arriving shoebill landed the other would fly straight off. The parents changed at the nest once in the morning and once in the afternoon, staying on average six hours each.

On the 30th of May, the first shoebill hatched. A tiny little grey bundle of down emerged, standing four inches high. On the 5th of June the second egg hatched, producing another bundle of grey fluff. The two parents were immensely proud of their young, they hurried around and gathered large quantities of reeds which they padded round the chicks. The parents never left them alone for even a few minutes. Until the chicks are two months old they are extremely vulnerable to birds of prey or crocodiles. Because of these predators, the majority of shoebill eggs and chicks never reach maturity.

Often, in turn, the birds walked off a short way and pulled up a mouthful of grass, which was then added to the nest. The male was standing at the nest and the female, on returning with the wet grass, brushed against his chest while she placed the wet grass around the chick. She then started to sway with her head lowered towards the chick, rubbing the male's chest. The male, like any male subjected to similar treatment, seemed to be acutely conscious of her actions. He started to stretch himself upwards and was getting excited, to say the least. It was difficult to judge how deliberate the female's behaviour was. She appeared to be absorbed by the chick, or was she? The male was standing as tall as he could, his eyes large and round and his beak slightly open. I thought that he was about to mount the female, but suddenly he took a step back, contact was broken, and he shrank back to his normal size. After a few moments he flew off and the female remained in attendance at the nest. Passion was apparently spent.

For the first two to three weeks the tiny chicks did not move an inch except to feed. The parents would gently push them back with their huge feet into the centre of the nest if they moved too near the edge.

I sat and watched the shoebill nest on average four or five days a week. I like to think my presence at the nest kept away unwelcome guests like the crocodiles, monitor lizards, and birds of prey. Even so, when the chicks were about three weeks old, I arrived at the nest one early morning and could only find one chick. I hunted about for the second chick but never found any trace of it. I could only guess what had happened. Either a predator had taken it, or it was possible that the parents may have dealt with it themselves. It was obvious as the surviving chick grew up that the parents simply could not have fed two of them. The demand for food was too great. The chicks fed on catfish for the first six weeks. The parents regurgitated the catfish whole, they would crush the fish up in their beaks, and then hold it tightly and lower their heads down to the chicks. The young would peck away at the crushed fish. One chick required on average six fish, or three fish and three water snakes a day. Each adult required at least the same again to keep itself going, so to have to feed a second chick would have been almost impossible. I was disappointed that the second chick had disappeared, as this seemed to be the only nest with two of them.

The chick which had survived all the dangers of the wild so far kept his parents very busy. For the first month the regurgitated catfish were headless. In the second month, when the chick had grown to a foot high and was sitting on the back of his knees, the catfish were regurgitated whole and swallowed without any hesitation by the large infant. It was also about this time that snake was added to the menu. These were small water snakes about two feet long, dark green on the back and bright yellow underneath. Snakes and catfish were the sole diet of the shoebill chick.

Watching the shoebills stalking and catching fish was marvellous entertainment. I have never seen any bird get into quite such chaos and confusion over what one would expect to be a simple task. They stalked very much like any other stork, walking with measured care, deftly placing their feet at every step, any movement of the body minimal, movement of the head nil. The eyes stared with only the occasional blink, peering through the vegetation into the water below. A slight movement of the prey would be spotted, then the head and neck would be thrust forward, tensed to pounce. Suddenly the bird would let fly at the passing fish or snake. It would virtually throw itself into the water head first, wings outstretched for balance. I saw, on numerous occasions, a shoebill losing its balance altogether and falling over on to one side or the other, using its wing as a prop. Shoebills lack the long, sharp beak of the other storks, who can neatly and easily select their victim and stab it. The huge size of the shoebill's beak means that when it grabs a fish it also grabs large clumps of reeds and volumes of water. It then has a struggle sorting the food out from the other material. Finally it does manage to swallow the fish, and then spits out the grass. It then has to have a long drink to help the fish down. Quite a carry on.

Both parents watched all birds of prey with keen interest. They tilted their heads sideways and stared up, watching hawks and eagles until they flew into the distance. Birds of prey seem to be the main predators, I would suspect the greatest danger of all. Crocodiles and monitor lizards were a danger but, thanks to the thick vegetation surrounding the nest, I had little fear that my remaining chick would be taken.

After a time the chick also began to watch the birds of prey like his parents. Should a lechwe or sitatunga approach the area, the adult shoebills would defend their chick courageously with a lot of beak-clapping. I imagine, although I never saw it, that shoebills would probably attack any animal if it actually came near the nest, charging with outstretched wings and clapping beaks, which ought to make anything turn and run.

I was surprised when I realized that the parents, after the first month, continued collecting water and pouring it over the chicks, just as they had with the eggs. This apparently cooled the chicks as well as giving them a few drops of water to drink. Their aim as they dropped the water was not very accurate, but several times the full amount, about a pint, would fall directly on top of the chicks, drenching them. Their little faces seemed to register surprise as rivulets of water ran round their eyes, dripping from the end of their beaks and running off their backs. But after a month the remaining chick was spared this treatment. The parents would collect water, carry it back to the chick, and allow it to drip slowly from their closed beaks for the chick to swallow.

In the early days of drenching, this method did not appear to be enough to keep the chicks cool in the harsh midday sun, and they had to be protected and shaded by their parents who sat on them when they were very young. But in the second month the remaining chick was too big to sit on, so the parents positioned themselves between him and the sun. In the third month, the parents decided that he was old enough to look after himself and must learn to tolerate the heat, although on exceptionally hot windless days the chick would still creep into the shadow made by his parents.

So the little chick started to grow, and to look like a miniature shoebill. At twenty-three days he began to preen. I could not yet see any feathers, but obviously they were coming and the chick was apparently scratching away at his baby down to make way for them. Also at that time he started to stagger to the edge of the nest on his 'knees' to relieve himself. This was the first journey in his life. Until that time he had remained rooted to the middle of the nest, lying down flat except when he raised his head to feed. But even when staggering along on his knees, he was still liable to fall flat on his nose. He remained on his knees until he was in his ninth week, when he made a huge effort and raised himself to his feet. He stood nearly three feet high, rather unsteadily, with stubby little wings outstretched to help keep his balance. In this way he managed to reach the edge of the nest, relieve himself and stagger back to collapse once again. It surprised me that at nine weeks old he was still so unsteady on his feet, and could not stay upright for more than half a minute.

To go back to his fifth week, at thirty-six days old to be precise, the first little feathers began to appear and he then started to use his preening gland. The preening gland is at the lower end of the back, which was then still covered by down. He would stretch back his head and gently squeeze the preening gland with his beak for the oil which would waterproof his feathers. With the oil smeared on the tip of his beak, he would then run through each of his tiny feathers. The oil acted not only as waterproofing, but perhaps at other times of the year to provide warmth. The fifth and sixth weeks showed distinct behavioural growth. The chick started to sit up more on his knees and began to become aware of his surroundings, watching the ever-dreaded birds of prey like his parents. He would peer around the nest for any old tit-bit, move around on his 'knees' and even started to shift and re-arrange some of the nesting material.

The first feathers appeared on his wings, then a few on his back, and later during the ninth and tenth weeks they started to appear on his neck and head. The absurd tuft of feathers displayed by his parents started to emerge in the tenth week. Soon the feathers on his wings were maturing. The same growth followed on his back, but the skin under his wings was still covered with down. He still had a lot of down on his chest and the unfeathered part of his back.

I was interested to see the female lie down in the nest with her chick. It was a squeeze with the two of them, but they just managed it. The chick would sometimes sit on its knees to preen or just to look around, and would then tower over its mother who lay with her eyes tightly shut. One morning two pied crows hovered overhead, and started to dive bomb them for a short while, causing them much annoyance. The shoebills raised their heads and opened their beaks in a threatening gesture, and the crows soon got bored with the game and flew off.

During the tenth week, faint markings were also beginning to appear on the chick's beak. Born with a little grey beak with no markings, I could see yellowish patches appearing and the grey was growing darker. The adult male was now less reluctant to leave the nest. The chick was considered old and big enough to be left for short periods, while the male went a few hundred yards away to fish. As soon as he had caught something he would return to the nest and regurgitate either a catfish or snake. The female rarely left the home and usually remained sitting or standing at the nest.

One sunny morning, with what seemed in the tropics a bitter wind blowing, I had just settled down in my canoe after setting up the equipment. I heard a slight movement behind me and on turning saw to my surprise Lady Shoebill slowly creeping up on me, apparently to take a closer look. I sat quietly and took a few photographs of her. She came to within six feet of the canoe and stood and stared at me for ten minutes while I sat and stared back. I could not help smiling with admiration at her courage and trust. After all that time, this was a very moving encounter and one which I shall never forget.

During the months of July and August my filming suffered badly from smoke haze. The local inhabitants, who live on islands in the swamp, burn the long, dry grass to make way for new growth and to improve the grazing. The sky was full of smoke which reduced the light by 1½*f* stops. When I was using long lenses this was a problem. The whole area was terribly dry by then and with a strong wind blowing continuously, it meant that most of the fires got out of control, roaring along at a terrifying rate, destroying all in their path. The remarkable thing was that after only two days of fire, fresh green grass could be seen struggling up through the hard, parched soil.

The chick's last month in the nest saw rapid development. The parents would now leave the chick for long periods while they both went off fishing. Sometimes I could see both parents fishing about five hundred yards away. Whoever was officially in attendance at the nest would fly back to the chick as soon as he or she had caught something. Up to the very last day of watching the family, the chick was still having to be fed, and always pecked at his parents' beaks begging for more.

Soon feathers appeared in the last few areas where down remained. Every time the chick preened in these areas (neck, head and chest) a thin stream of down would be caught by the wind and carried away. Definite markings on his beak increased and the tuft of feathers on his head grew more noticeable day by day. It was in the eleventh week that he started to stand on his feet. But he was very shaky and his knees would start to tremble after a few moments. He used his wings to help keep his balance. As each day passed his strength increased until during the thirteenth and fourteenth weeks he was able to stand, walk and jump a little, without actually losing balance and falling flat on his face.

It was in the fourteenth week that I found the chick six feet away from the nest, lying in a clump of reeds. I got quite a shock finding an empty nest, as I had got so used to seeing him there over four months. Terrible thoughts raced through my mind. But, keeping calm, I found him quickly enough, and was able to manoeuvre my canoe round him to film and photograph. From that day on the chick regularly moved about, straying further and further from the nest. By the fifteenth week he would walk over to a clump of reeds and then sit down in the middle of it almost totally hidden. Only because I knew the shoebills so well by now was I able to pick out his outline in the tall grass. Having rested he would venture out once more, and walk into the open, stopping every now and then to peer into the water. Then he would seek security in the next clump of tall reeds. By the sixteenth week, my final week with him, he joined his parents and walked around with them. He could now fly, and walk through the long grass and keep his balance, but he was still dependent on his parents for food. All three never left the nest area, and were always within a thousand yards of it.

During the final week with my shoebill family I studied the young bird to see how he differed from his parents. By now he was as tall as his mother, but darker in colour. He could fly nearly as well, could walk as well, but still could not feed himself. The markings on his beak were not as distinct as those of his parents, but the tuft on his head was just as pronounced.

On one occasion the male regurgitated a huge catfish which fell into the bottom of the nest. Instead of consuming it the young bird just sat and gazed down at it, making his hunger noise. After a few moments he half-heartedly pecked at the fish, then tried to pick it up and play with it. I was puzzled and could not see why the chick would not swallow the fish. Perhaps it was too big. He continued to play with the fish for ten minutes, making his hunger noises and looking up at his parent with a plaintive expression, until suddenly father grabbed the fish, swallowed it again, and walked off to have a drink. The infant had to learn the hard way.

On my last day in the swamps I managed to get my airboat stuck for three and a half hours on an island that was nearly dry. During my long and tiring struggle to free myself Lady Shoebill suddenly took to the air in the distance and flew towards me. I felt a lump in my throat. I stopped pushing to watch where she would go.

She actually landed twenty feet away, and then once again

calmly and sedately walked up to within six feet without any hesitation. She stood and stared at me for nearly twenty minutes, while I sat exhausted and panting on the front of the airboat. Neither of us moved or uttered.

I like to believe that she had come to say farewell. We had been together for five long months in the sun, rain, cloud and smoke, and she had always been the one who tolerated me best. This touching interlude was a rewarding sequel to a long, hard struggle.

SEVEN

Elephant Valley

It was on an earlier visit to Zambia that I had first heard of the Luangwa Valley and had spent two nights on the Luangwa River, camping with Norman Carr, a famous and lovable character who is also a distinguished naturalist.

It was the dry season and the river was very low, with many sandbanks, and what seemed from the air only a trickle of water winding through them. Nevertheless I could also see hundreds of hippos wallowing in the pools.

South Luangwa National Park, as it is known, is the second largest wildlife reserve in Zambia. Established in 1972, it had formerly been a game reserve. It is over nine thousand square kilometres and very popular with tourists, mostly from Southern Africa, because of its great variety of animals and birds. It is well known for the exceptional number of elephants, estimated at over a hundred thousand, as well as buffalo, hippo, impala, puku, zebra, waterbuck, warthogs and crocodiles. Cookson's wildebeest occur in fair numbers only in the Luangwa valley, along with Thornicroft's giraffe, of which there are probably not more than five hundred in the world. Lion, leopard and cheetah are numerous, birdlife is prolific, one of the main attractions being the carmine bee-eaters which nest in huge colonies in the river banks.

We went out for our first tour with a young warden, Phil Berry, one of the leading experts on the Luangwa Valley. For several years he had worked for the Game Department, patrolling the valley in the dry and wet seasons. His great love is the Thornicroft's giraffe, which he was studying.

It was not the giraffes that fascinated me, but the carmine bee-eaters. I hoped that these exquisite birds could be included in a film in the context of the Luangwa River and Valley. Phil showed us a small colony of a few hundred nesting in the river bank, and gave me some useful information about their habits.

The Luangwa Valley is about fifty miles wide, with the river snaking down the centre, in some parts about two hundred yards wide. For a mile or more either side of the river there is a lush green belt of trees, bushes and grass but beyond that the scene opens up and becomes very bare.

Phil drove me to Norman Carr's camp which was built right on the edge of the river bank, and made entirely of grass and mopani poles. Norman Carr himself came through the fading light to greet us, an elderly man, small, wiry, with a face deeply tanned from years under the African sun. He had a stoop and I heard later that his back had been broken when he was tossed by a buffalo.

We were shown our little grass huts and after a shower and a change of clothes we sat down to a meal under the stars. As we were talking peacefully, an elephant quietly walked right into the camp.

Norman was the first to notice the visitor and told us all to keep quiet, relax and just watch. The elephant was an old bull who was apparently used to the camp and its inmates. He walked carefully through a gap in the grass fence and wandered around the camp with his trunk trailing on the ground, looking for tit-bits. He was careful not to tread on anything or brush too near the fragile grass huts. He was in no way threatening. He stayed in the camp for half an hour and then quietly left through the same gap in the fence and disappeared into the night.

Next morning Norman took us around in an open Land-

Rover to see as much as possible of the valley in the brief time available. We saw two bee-eater colonies one of which had about seven hundred nests. We sat down for a while and watched a wonderful sight. A thousand dazzling birds took off together, wheeling above the banks and then descending again and disappeared into their tunnels.

I felt sure that the changing spectacle of the Luangwa Valley would make an interesting film and before leaving arranged with Norman to come back for another reconnaissance.

After a second quick visit to make detailed plans with Norman I returned in May 1976 to begin serious filming. I decided to build my own establishment with local labour at the southern end of the Carr camp, right on the top of the river bank. It consisted of a grass hut with a veranda for myself, a separate shower and loo, another hut divided into a kitchen and store, and a smaller grass hut for anyone who came to visit me. Finally a six foot grass fence surrounded the whole camp, and it took only about a week to finish.

During the two years I spent in the valley I had one boy, with the surprising name of Patterson Wandilla, whose job was to look after my camp while I was out filming. He made my bed, washed my clothes, heated the water and made sure everything was clean and tidy. Patterson was small and muscular and spoke a smattering of English and was always smiling. If I needed a guard to accompany me in the bush, I would take one of the other boys from the camp. I carried my camera and the boy carried my rifle, for if we came face to face with a lion, leopard, buffalo, rhino, or elephant, I wanted to do the filming rather than the shooting.

Although I never got attacked by anything myself, Patterson was badly bitten by a burrowing viper. And during 1976, one of the hunters I knew was attacked by a lion in the long grass. The hunter shot the lion four times but each time it fell to the ground it got up again. It eventually grabbed the hunter by the right ankle and savagely tore at him before falling dead at his feet. The poor hunter lost his right leg below the knee.

I also saw two Africans who had been attacked by wild animals. One had been mauled by a lion and the other tossed by a buffalo. The one mauled had been savaged in the middle of the night. A lioness had pounced on the unfortunate man, grabbing him by his thigh. The hunter for whom the African worked finally arrived on the scene with his rifle and slowly approached the lioness, walking nearer and nearer. Only when the hunter was ten feet from the lioness did she finally drop the struggling man. The hunter shot her in the head.

The other African had been tossed by a buffalo. He had been walking through the bush in fairly long grass from one village to another when he had come face to face with a buffalo. Both had given each other an awful fright and the buffalo had charged past the man catching him in the stomach with one of its horns.

I loved the valley, and enjoyed every day of the two years I was to spend there. I had my ups and downs, but the downs were quickly forgotten. Usually I would get up at five-thirty and after a quick cup of tea, I left camp by six not returning until six in the evening. A canvas water bottle was all I needed, sometimes a biscuit or two.

The first month was, I admit, a bit nerve wracking. Sometimes driving around on my own, I would find myself surrounded by elephants or buffalo, rhino or lions, and my heart beat overtime. This was because I did not yet know the animals well enough, or what any of them would do next. But after a while, when I began to understand their behaviour and could judge if an animal was getting upset or nervous, I became more relaxed myself. I began to understand which animal I could approach without danger of upsetting it. For instance, I could approach a lone bull elephant very near to get a close-up on film, with little chance of him charging me.

Even if he did, the chances were that it would only be a mock performance, not the real thing. But it would be very unwise to approach a cow elephant with young, as she would feel very protective and would certainly charge if she felt threatened. A family group of elephants could also be approached more closely, although one always had to keep an eye on the dominant female, as she would charge if she thought the group was at risk.

I always enjoyed occasional walks through the bush with a guard. The whole time I was looking and listening, especially under the scrub to make sure a lion was not close by, in the grass in case one stepped on a snake, in the trees in case a leopard was ready to spring. At any slight noise one would stop, straining eyes and ears. Was it an elephant, or a rhino, or only a baboon? To stalk animals on foot one advances up wind, as in that way I could get close enough to film. One sniff of human scent and they would be off. Never once during the two years in the valley did I or my guard have to fire a shot in self defence, whether into the air or at an animal. I was pleased about this, but I came near to it once or twice.

On one such occasion I had been working in a particular area, trying to find some giraffe that had been reported there, when I came across a young bull elephant, probably about fifteen or twenty years old. I noted that he was limping badly, whenever he stopped he would lift his right front leg. I was in the car, and drove up as near as I could without scaring him, and had a close look at the leg through the binoculars. It was a horrible sight, as it had been caught in a poacher's wire snare. The elephant had managed to break the wire, which had probably been secured to a tree, but the coil was still round his ankle. It had cut through the skin and tightened round the bone, while six feet of loose wire was being dragged along behind. There was no doubt that the poor animal was in great pain, lifting his leg off the ground whenever he stopped, and halting at most water holes and small streams to suck up water into his trunk and letting it dribble slowly over the horribly swollen and infected leg. I reported the incident to Phil Berry who sent a message to the Game Department to send someone up to shoot the wretched creature and put it out of its misery. It took a week for a game guard to turn up and deal with it, and a whole week of misery for the elephant. This was bureaucracy at its worst. Apparently the Game Department could not give permission to someone sensible like Phil Berry to shoot it. It had to be an accredited official.

The elephant was finally tracked down and put out of its misery, when it was shot alongside a little stream falling backwards into the water. However macabre, I knew that in a few days, when the meat had softened in the water and gone rotten the crocodiles would come and have a huge feast. So after a few days I drove back and parked the car half a mile from where the carcase lay. I had with me a game guard carrying my rifle, and with my cameras we set off slowly and quietly up-stream. After a few hundred yards we came across a hippo out in the bush. Usually hippos spend the day in water, sleeping and keeping cool, only coming out at night to feed on the grass. But for some reason this hippo was wandering about feeding during the day. Happily there was a convenient ant-hill nearby, twenty feet high, up which we clambered until the hippo had moved on.

We continued upstream until I could just hear some splashing in the stream. I reckoned the crocs had found the elephant and had already begun to feed. We advanced stealthily, avoiding any twigs, stopping to listen and watch as the splashing grew louder. Finally we reached the spot where the noise was coming from, so I put down my cameras and dropped to my hands and knees. Indicating to my guard that I wanted him to stay where he was, I crawled to the edge of the bank and peered over. There were at least fifty crocs thrashing about in the water tearing meat off the dead elephant. Some had managed to get right inside the elephant, and the whole carcase was jumping about in the water. A croc would get hold of a piece of flesh and twirl itself round in the water, over and over, until the joint was twisted off. Then it would raise its head and swallow.

I was totally engrossed watching the crocs only ten feet below me, when all of a sudden, to my left and very close, there was a huge roar. I whipped round and saw to my horror no less than six lionesses not twenty feet from me. They were lying down, and had also been watching the crocodiles, perhaps wishing they could share the elephant feast. I had been so quiet in my approach to the river that none of the great cats had heard me coming, and had only spotted me when I crawled to the edge of the river bank.

That first roar almost gave me heart failure. I remember wondering whether to dive into the river and have a battle against the crocs, or stand my ground and take my chance with the lions. But I just stayed rooted to the spot, stopped breathing, and prayed that the lions would just go away. Thank goodness I had given the lions as much of a fright as they had given me, and suddenly they all jumped to their feet, making ugly growling noises, and dashed off into the bush.

I watched them disappear, and almost immediately several elephants nearby began to trumpet in alarm. The lions, in their fright, had run into a small group of elephants. These in turn had blundered off, crashing through anything and everything. Every form of wildlife in the area was now disturbed. I do not recall much else. I think I simply closed my eyes and tried hard to calm my thumping head and heart. In due course I turned and saw my guard, rifle loaded and safety catch off, staring into the bush where the lionesses had disappeared. If it had been possible, I think he might even have looked a little pale. I looked back over the bank and was not surprised to find that all the crocs had disappeared, so I picked up my cameras and tottered back to the car. I went back again next day, first making sure no dangerous animal was hiding nearby, and filmed the crocs finishing off the elephant.

I was occasionally chased by elephants in my car, but that was no problem as I could easily get away. Being chased by an elephant when I was on foot was a different matter. Then I broke some world records. I was once chased by a hippo. I was at the edge of a lagoon getting close-ups of two hippos in the water. Usually hippos feel quite safe in water, but that day one of them took immediate exception to me. It suddenly reared up and came at me at an incredible speed, ploughing through three feet of water with its vast mouth wide open. I do not pretend to be brave. I abandoned my tripod and camera, bounded like a cheetah to the nearest tree and went up it in a matter of seconds. The hippo stopped beneath me for a few minutes while I clung to the flimsy branches of the thorn tree, and then mercifully got bored and wandered back into the lagoon. To this day, I have no idea how I got up that tree, because it took me all of twenty minutes to get down again. It was practically impenetrable.

Early in my stay I had seen several groups of elephants crossing the river in the evenings. The west side of the river is National Park and the east side a hunting area. The elephants get to know that during the day the Park is safe, but during the night the hunting areas are equally safe and more food is available there. So they cross over. As soon as dawn breaks the groups move back to the river and quickly return to the Park before any hunters appear.

I wanted to film these early crossings. It meant getting up at four, driving in darkness to one of the main crossing points, setting up equipment and waiting. The elephants, in groups of between ten and twenty, usually crossed back into the Park before light. This was no good for filming, so whenever I could hear the elephants gathering to cross the river I would flash my headlights, clap my hands and shout to frighten them back into the bush. If the elephants were desperate to cross, all they had to do was go up or down stream and cross at another point. But sometimes they went back into the bush, waited half an hour or so and tried again. I hoped there would be sufficient light by then for me to film them as they almost ran across, lifting their trunks to pick up any scent, knowing that they were late and time was pressing.

I concentrated mainly on the river life. It is said that there are about forty hippos to every mile of river, and about the same number of crocodiles making an impressive total over four hundred miles of river. I spent much time watching and filming hippos, especially the young. Like their mothers, they sleep during the day in the river, resting their chins on a sandbank or on their mother's back. I filmed one young hippo climbing on its mother's back, pink feet exposed, and then falling into a blissful sleep.

Hippos live in small herds. Thirty seems an average number with a dominant male in charge. The dominant male will fight off any other who dares to intrude. These battles are sometimes vicious, as I had seen some time before on Lake Naivasha. The males charge each other, teeth bared, rearing up on their hind legs, trying to bite with their huge teeth. In one fight which I filmed, one male chased another on to the sandbanks, and they then chased each other all round the place for some minutes before going back into the river at full speed, sending spray ten feet into the air. Sometimes these savage battles end in death. As always it does not take the crocodiles long to find a dead hippo, and as many as two hundred crocs may tear one animal to pieces, leaving no trace after two days. Nearly every hippo, especially the males, show ugly scars on the backs and sides from numerous skirmishes.

There were many puku, delicate antelopes, living along the banks of the Luangwa and I filmed two wild dogs attacking a young one by the river. It happened early one morning. I was parked right by the river filming elephants crossing from the hunting areas. I had seen a fairly large herd of puku walk out of some grass and wander down over the sand to take their

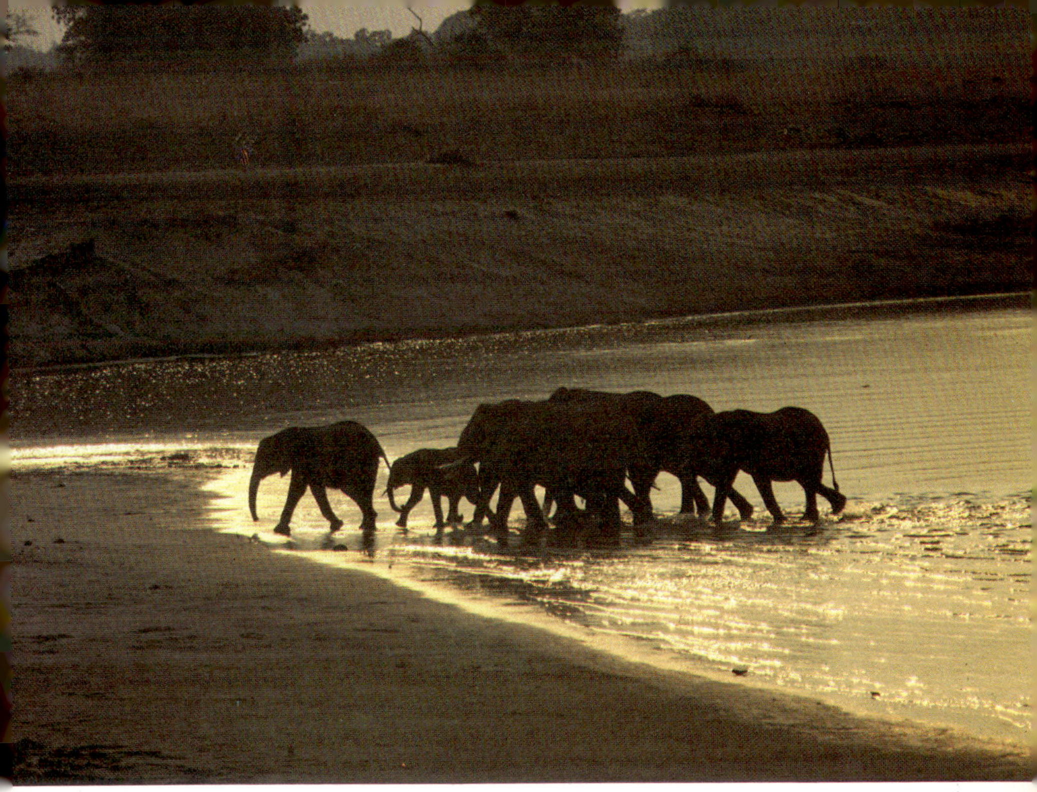

Crossing the Luangwa River at dawn.

Peaceful hippo with oxpeckers.

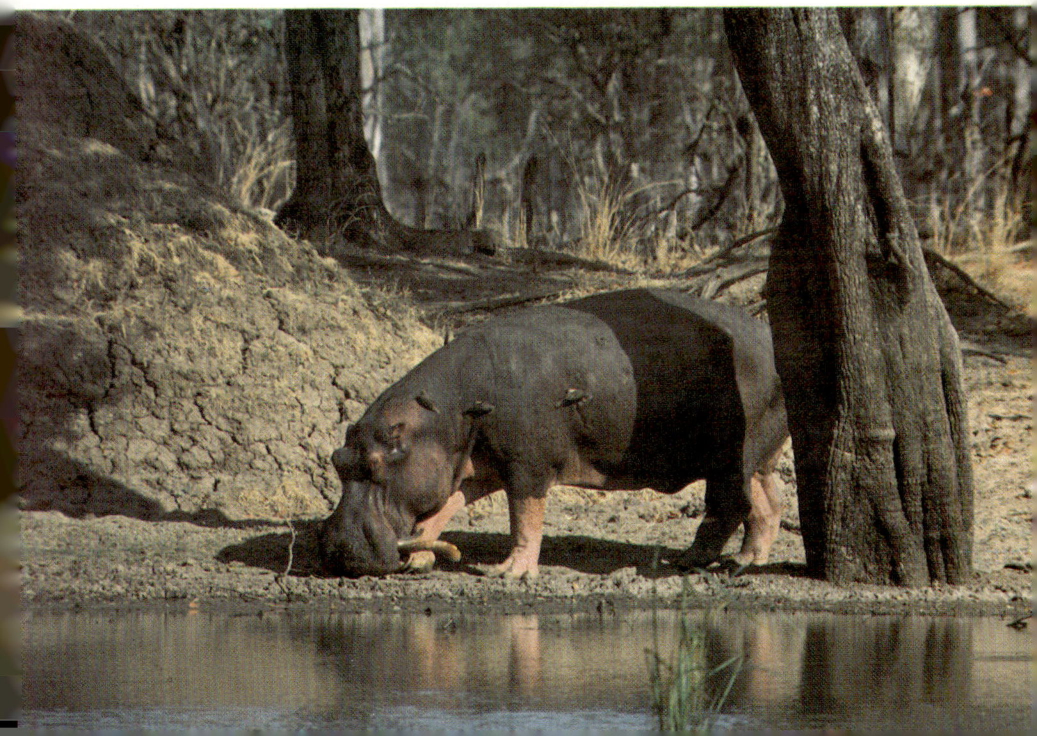

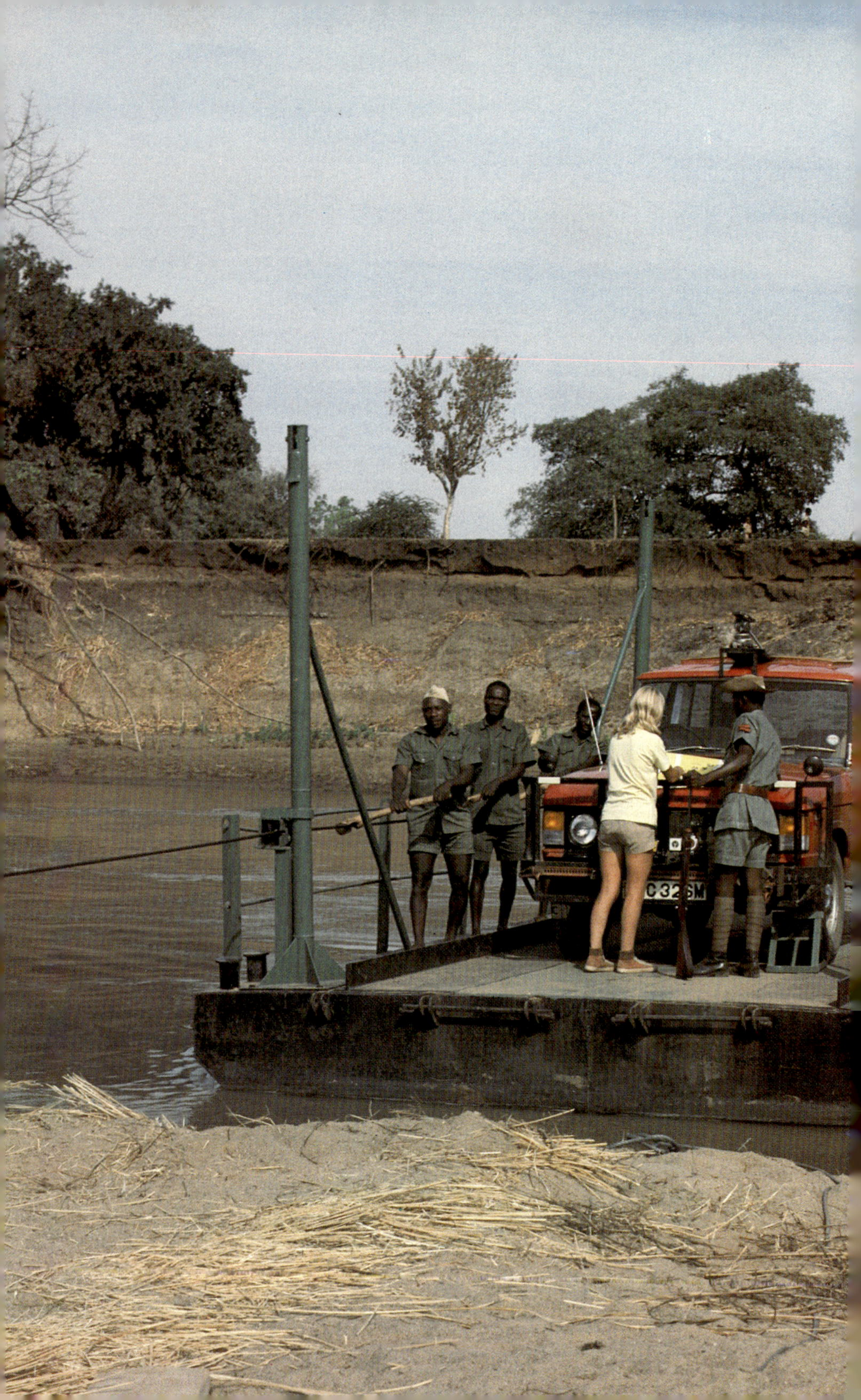

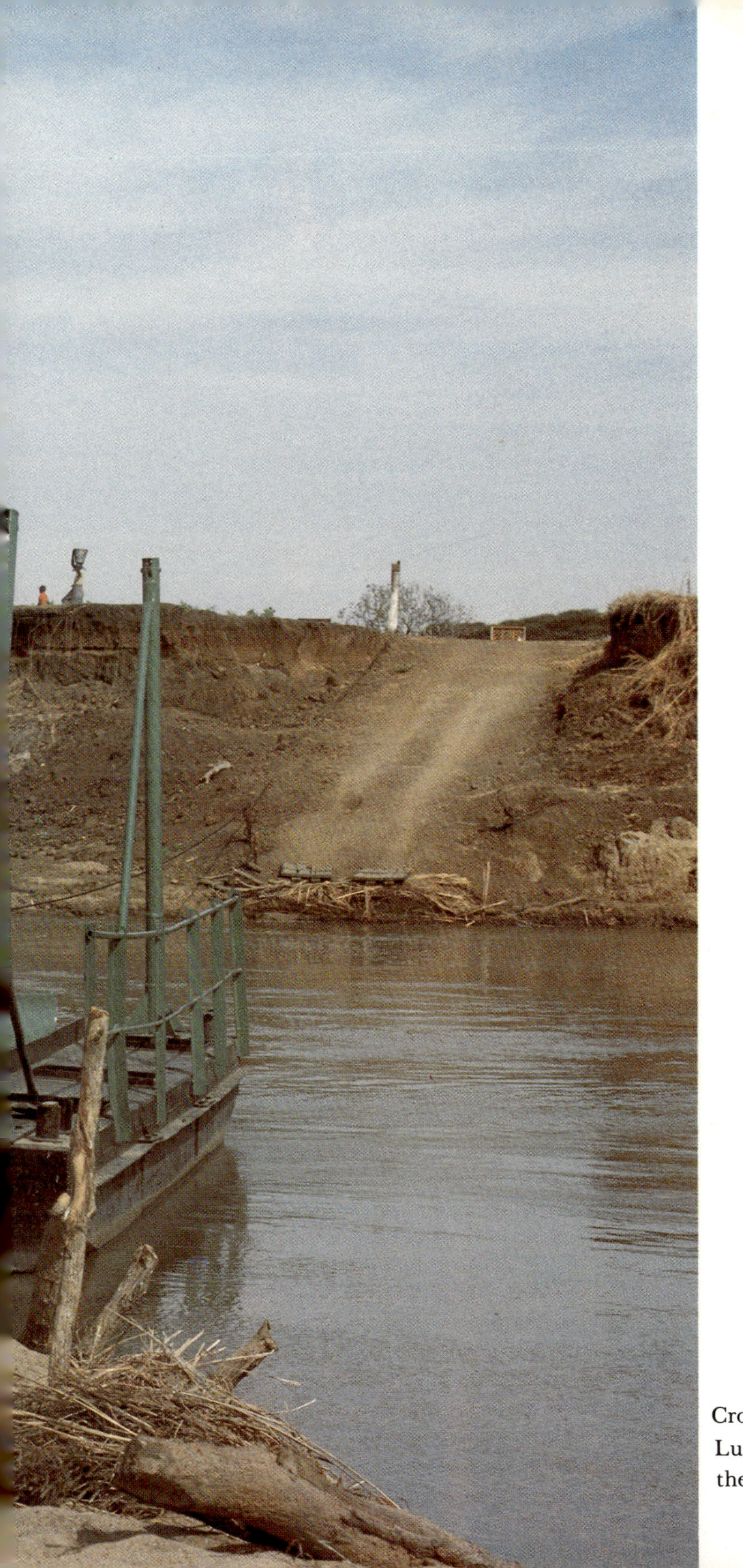

Crossing the
Luangwa River in
the midday sun.

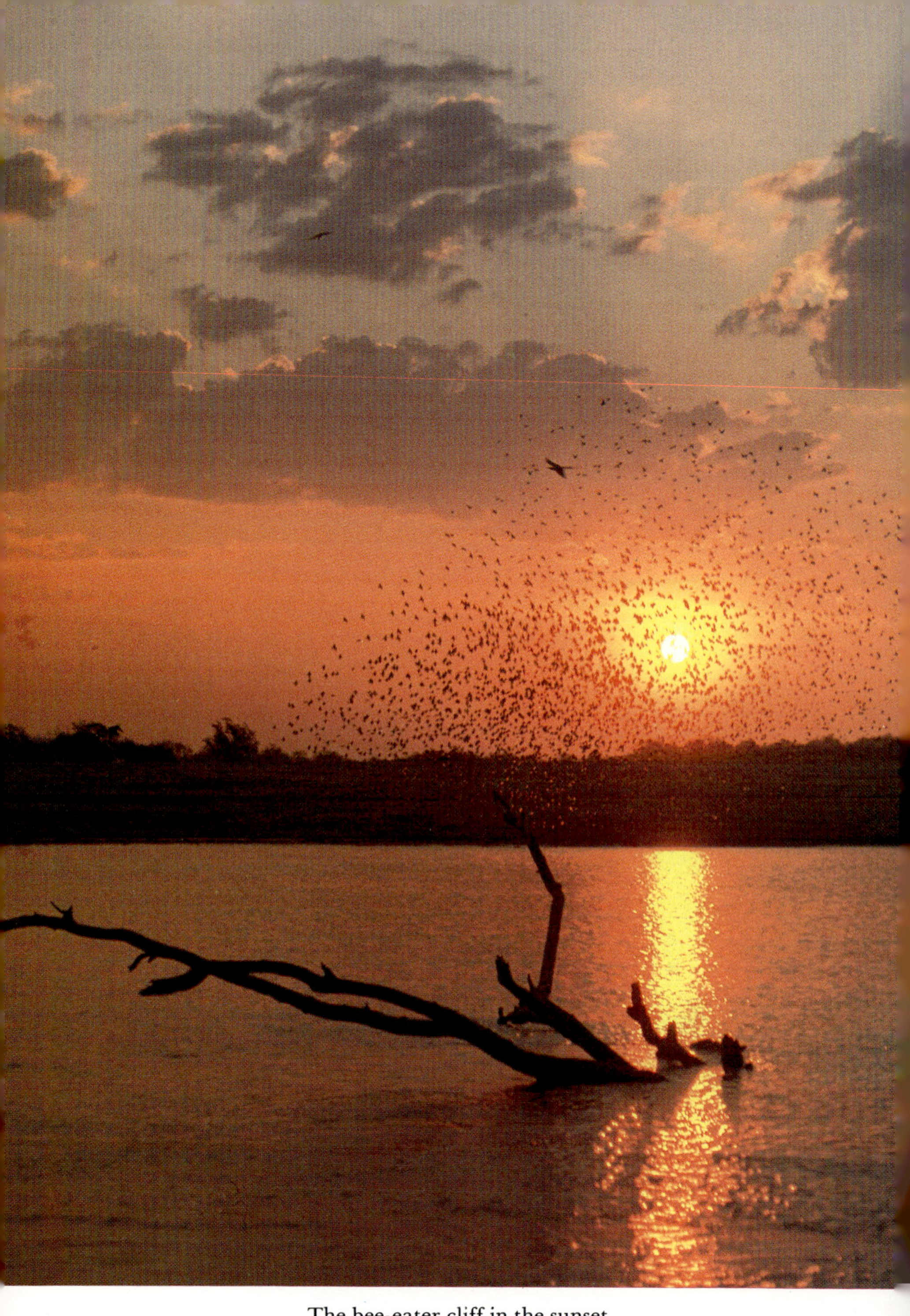

The bee-eater cliff in the sunset.

first morning drink. It was a lovely peaceful sight, with the sun catching the orange dust as it rose over the herd. All seemed quiet, but suddenly some of the older puku sounded their alarm whistle and turned round to face the grass from where they had emerged. I thought that maybe a lion was coming, but I was wrong, for two wild dogs came racing out of the grass straight for the herd. All hell broke loose and the puku spurted into a gallop. Fortunately, most of them came my way, so that puku and dogs both passed within fifty feet. The dogs suddenly stopped and stood still, watching the herd of puku wheel away. I thought that maybe they had given up, but suddenly one dog shot off into the long grass and flushed out a young puku crouching there. The other dog then rushed in and grabbed the puku by the hind leg while the other caught it somewhere up front. I do not know how the puku managed it, but suddenly it broke free from both dogs and galloped off, hotly pursued. The dogs ran into the long grass and I momentarily lost them through the lens, but picked them up again for a few seconds before they once again disappeared.

I snatched up my small camera and ran into the long grass. The two dogs were right on the edge of the river looking down at a commotion in the water ten feet below. I realized immediately what had happened. The young puku in panic and terror must have leapt straight over the bank into the river and into the jaws of a dozing ten foot crocodile. I filmed the crocodile swimming downstream with the dead puku in its mouth.

EIGHT

Flood

As time went on I was able to watch and film the cycle of the changing seasons at Luangwa about which Norman had told me so much.

From mid-March, when the river begins to drop, to mid-July it was winter; it was cold at night, and frosts have been known. By day it was warm, with clear blue skies. The animal population of the valley is widely scattered at that period, as there is ample food throughout the valley. All the small rivers and water holes are full. From August to November it gets increasingly hot. The rivers and water holes start to dry up and the food supply becomes more scarce. The grass and bushes become brown and burnt. Then from November to March torrents of rain fall which cause the smaller rivers to flood and sometimes make the Luangwa overflow its banks and swamp large areas of the valley floor.

In order to help me film the changing seasons at Luangwa in the 1977 season, my friend Bill Barclay several times sent up his Cessna 206, so that I could take aerial shots of the valley. It was a lovely change to fly over the wide valley floor, searching for animals, seeing whether the lagoons, water holes and small rivers had dried up, viewing huge concentrations of hippos in the river, and just flying here and there. With Bill's 206 I could take off the two loading doors and strap myself in securely so that I could sit right over the edge of the aircraft. The pilot was careful not to bank too sharply in case I fell out.

At one point I also hired a small helicopter so that I could hover over certain scenes, particularly the lagoons, water holes and the thousands of animal tracks through the bush. We hovered over the big bush fires and if we saw a good rain storm coming, with big black clouds, I could get the pilot to move into the right position. It was a marvellous way to get around the valley and I often wished I was opulent enough to own my own plane and keep it in the valley. It would have made life a lot easier.

From April to August that year I filmed many predators and their victims. All the well-known predators can be found in the Luangwa. Wild dogs and hyenas roam in large numbers. Lions are there in abundance and some leopards. Although cheetah are known to occur in the valley I never saw one in two years.

I got on film a pride of lions, a total of eleven in all including a beautiful black-maned lion, six lionesses and their cubs about nine months old.

One day I was in my car getting close-ups of a fine male greater kudu with a magnificent set of horns. I knew this particular animal quite well as he had broken one of his hind legs some time before. Neither I nor anyone at Chibembe camp thought he would survive long. But we were wrong, for he lived nearly three months with his broken leg, hopping and staggering around on the other three. On this occasion I was parked not more than fifty feet away, filming him nibbling a bush, when he suddenly whirled around. I looked over my shoulder and saw three lionesses from the pride approaching. For a second I thought they were stalking me and my heart nearly stopped, but then I realized they were after the kudu and my camera started to roll.

The kudu watched the lionesses until they were only a hundred feet away, and then turned and ran on his three legs into the bush. Immediately the three lionesses broke into a fast trot. After the three leading animals came another three, these walking and panting in the heat. Then came the four bouncing cubs, stumbling over on the uneven ground and followed in a stately fashion by the male. They all passed my open vehicle not more than thirty feet away, glancing in my direction as they passed. Happily they were more interested in the kudu.

I started my Range Rover and tried desperately to keep up with the lions over the appalling ground, but it was impossible and I soon lost sight of them in the thick bush. When I eventually caught up they had already reduced the poor kudu to nothing but bare ribs, skull and legs, and were growling, pushing and taking occasional swipes at each other. Their bellies were bloated and eventually they could barely crawl over to a tree, which offered some shade and where they could all lie down and sleep off the meal.

If life out in the bush was not exciting enough, life in camp always had surprises in store. The vervet monkeys were always around in the trees, playing and chasing each other from branch to branch. When they thought I was not looking they would sneak down and wander round the camp searching for food or for anything to pinch. My camp boy was always chasing the monkeys away. From camp I could see the hippos lying on the sandbanks in the sun.

From August to November I was visited nearly every night by two or three elephants. I would be woken up any time between eleven at night and four in the morning by loud tearing sounds. It was always the elephants outside my six foot grass fence. They would lean on it and it would finally tear and fall apart and the elephants would then walk through. The first time this happened I nearly died of fright and barricaded myself inside my flimsy hut, burying myself under the bed clothes. The elephants passed a few feet away and I could hear their deep, heavy breathing and their tummies rumbling.

After a few weeks I got used to this routine and learned

that they were very careful not to tread on anything. They made no attempt to touch my hut. I would sometimes get out of bed, sit on the veranda and watch the huge animals wander round camp eating the bushes and trees but carefully walking round my tables, chairs and the car. Sometimes I tried to stop them coming in by flashing a torch into their eyes, clapping or shouting, and they would then leave, flattening yet another part of my fence on the way out.

One elephant in particular got so used to me that after a while he took absolutely no notice and just went on eating. I decided to take a few photographs, using a flash. I was not too sure how he would react. The flash gave the elephant a fright and he whipped round and flapped his ears. I retreated behind my car. He left camp that night but came back the next. After a few weeks I was able to walk within fifteen feet of him, right out in the open and take photographs without him even stopping eating.

From about August onwards, once the main sandbanks have dried out, the crocodiles excavate their nest holes. Usually set back a hundred feet or so from the water, the croc digs two or three feet deep and lays as many as forty-five eggs. Covering it all afterwards, the female will sit over the nest during part of the day to keep the eggs cool and also to protect them from intrusion. Monitor lizards love crocs' eggs and constantly search the sandbanks for them. Finding the eggs apparently by smell, the monitor digs them out and eats as many as it can manage.

If the eggs survive raids by monitors, they ultimately hatch. The tiny young crocs, only four inches long, have to struggle through the sand to the surface and then find their way to the river without assistance from parents or anyone else. Only a percentage of tiny crocs survive to maturity.

The locals did find two nests for me. Hides were built, and I spent days watching the nests, either for crocs to come and sit on them, or for monitors to make a raid. But sadly I drew a blank. Nothing whatever happened during the seven days I waited, cooped up and cramped in the hides.

The Luangwa River is famous for bee-eaters. The carmines arrive in the valley in July and August from the east coast of Africa, and begin to pair off and choose a suitable site for the great dig. The beautiful bright birds choose a straight stretch of bank, never a corner where the river might cut under it. Colonies range from a few dozen to several thousand nests. In July and August the birds dig frantically using beaks to peck at the sandy soil, and feet to push the loose sand out of the entrance. At the end of a long tunnel, three to eight feet long, from one to three white eggs are finally laid.

There is much communal display, while the bee-eaters dig throughout the day. At intervals the entire colony takes off, wheeling round the site a few times and then settling down again. In the evenings the birds mass in the trees by the river to roost. Before finally quietening down for the night they fly low over the water dipping themselves into the surface to wash off the sand.

Once the eggs have been laid both parents share the duties. While one is sitting, the other flies off to gather food on the wing. After hatching the hungry chicks, the parents hunt insects all day and bees are one of their favourite prey. I was told that the birds apparently squeeze the end of the bee to remove the sting before swallowing.

In September and October they are all tirelessly feeding young. Disaster strikes sometimes and it takes different forms. Bee-eaters seem to have two main enemies. The yellow-billed kite hovers over the colony to snatch any young that venture to a tunnel entrance. It might occasionally attempt to catch an adult bird. Then the monitor lizard constantly preys on the colony. It climbs the vertical river bank and digs its way into the colony, eating any eggs or chicks as it goes. I filmed one monitor on a raid. When it had finished its plundering and wanted to withdraw, several carmine bee-eaters attacked it.

Every time the monitor poked its head out of a tunnel, several birds dive-bombed, which caused the monitor to retreat inside again. It was half an hour before the monitor managed to escape.

The final threat to the bee-eater colonies are the banks themselves. I had seen how the natural rainfall of the previous year had damaged them, but now I noticed that the dry season could have the same effect. By October the ground is rock-hard, baked by months of scorching sun, and long deep cracks appear along the top of the banks. With all the bee-eaters' tunnels underneath, the banks are weak and sometimes collapse. Young chicks are buried along with adults caught in their tunnels, and many eggs are broken.

I built a hide at one of the colonies, made of grass and mopani poles set up tight against the bank in the middle of the colony. The birds soon accepted the hide and I was able to film some nice close-ups of the birds, digging, bringing food to the nests, and feeding their young. One morning I was walking along the bottom of the bank approaching my hide, when suddenly the bank above it collapsed. My hide was flattened and buried under several tons of rock-hard soil. In another few moments I would have been inside the hide. There was no way in which I could have emerged unscathed. I took no further risks.

When the temperature reaches up into the hundreds the birds have three ways of cooling down. They open their beaks, like a dog panting. Others sit on a perch and bend their heads right over to one side, opening up the neck feathers to allow what little air there is to penetrate to the skin. Or some may find a flat piece of ground, lie on their tummies and stretch their wings out to catch any cool air.

Bee-eaters were not the only creatures to find it hot. I once took a reading inside my hide and was amazed to find that the temperature was at 135°. I was not surprised because within a few minutes of entering the hide I was soaked through and perspiration ran down into my eyes.

In two bee-eater colonies I opened up part of the back to film inside the nesting chamber. I carefully stuck a very long reed down one of the tunnels until it hit the back of the nest. Having fixed the length I added a further three feet, and then dug a trench wide and deep enough for me and my camera. Slowly and carefully I excavated towards the back of the nests. When I had opened up the back of a nesting chamber, I inserted a pane of glass and covered it over with a piece of blanket to keep out the light. In one colony I opened up six nests which all had eggs, and then left the colony in peace for a week.

I wanted to film the eggs hatching, the parents feeding the young and the young growing. After a week I returned, installed my lights and cameras, and settled down. Filming an egg hatching was no problem. As soon as I noticed a hair-line crack I would sit glued to the camera until the egg hatched out. But the adult birds definitely did not like me, my cameras, and especially my lights. They were obviously reluctant to come into the nest to feed their young. I persevered in the hope that the birds would accept me, but in the end I was forced to leave them in peace for fear that they would desert their young.

The dry season was now several months on and the small rivers had long since dried up. I decided to drive up some of the river beds to see if I could find any signs of animals digging in the sand for water. It did not take long to find holes dug by elephants. They use their front feet to scoop out the sand, and if the water is far below the surface they have to kneel down to get at the water with their trunks. Once a hole has been dug, other animals use it and keep it open. I filmed elephants, warthogs, impala, baboons, bushbuck and others as well as birds and insects using the water holes in the dry river bed. I saw clear spoor marks of leopards using the water holes, but sadly never saw one.

Once I was hiding in the centre of a bush on the edge of a

dry river bed when suddenly I heard some deep heavy breathing. I peered round but could see nothing. Then I looked directly below, and not ten feet away was a male hippo. He had been walking slowly down the river bed, keeping right into the bank in the shade, which was why I had not seen him coming. I remained very still, for he was too close to film. Finally he moved on. He had a nasty wound on his side, a red gash a foot long and six inches wide, no doubt the result of a fight with a rival.

Another day I gave myself two healthy frights. First, as I was driving slowly in my open vehicle through the bush, I turned a corner and suddenly saw a pair of lions in front of me walking into the undergrowth. I stopped and waited for them to settle down in the shade. Then very slowly edged up to them until I was within thirty or forty feet. I gave my game guard a couple of soft-nosed bullets and started to film the lions. Suddenly the male, who had a fine ginger mane, leapt up, gave a loud growl and charged the open car. I heard the guard slip off the safety catch and at the same moment I actually shouted at the lion. To my surprise and relief it stopped dead in its tracks. I followed them for some time at a safe distance, filming them every fifteen minutes or so.

Later on that same day I found a small group of elephants walking through some mopani woodlands. I was able to get some nice footage of the group moving towards us through the trees shimmering in the heat haze. I had been careful to notice the line of the elephant path, so that they would pass close by me to the right. All went well until they got to within fifty feet. Instead of following their usual path they came straight for us.

I decided to stay put and film. The frame in my camera got fuller and fuller of elephants, and then only the head of an elephant was apparent. Finally all I could keep in the frame was the left eye of the leading cow. At that point she turned towards me, stopped and stared. Thank goodness the wind was in my favour. I got a useful shot of her glaring down into the camera. I think I had stopped breathing at this point, although my trusted game guard was behind me at the ready. I finally opened my other eye and judged that the elephants were ten feet from the other end of the car. Close enough. Once the leading female started to move off again, the rest of the herd slowly filed past us. I sat back and tugged at a cigarette.

The lagoons and water holes now began to dry up altogether. During the floods the fish in the river swim into the lagoons and water holes and then get marooned. The fish are quite happy, until the water drops to six inches or less. Then is the time for all the fish-eating birds to move in. Huge flocks of pelicans, herons, storks, fish-eagles, and of course the crocs and monitor lizards, all wade into the mud and feed on the fish. The fish are doomed and sometimes leap high out of the water to escape the predators. If the predators do not eat them all, the survivors are left in the soft mud, flapping about until the mud hardens around them and they bake in the sun. I once saw about forty fish-eagles swooping down on a small waterhole where hundreds of fish were trapped in the soft mud. Some of the fish were so big and heavy that the birds were unable to lift them. The fish-eagles fought each other over the prey although there was plenty for all.

Animals who by instinct are confined to their territories run a risk among the drying water holes. I found three different young animals trapped in the mud, a young wildebeest that was already dead and a young rhino and elephant that were both still alive. On both those occasions Phil Berry from Chibembe was with me, and he quickly summoned labour, ropes, spades and sacking. The first thing Phil did was to give water to the young animals and then put sacking over their heads to quieten them. It took a good two hours to dig each animal out, get ropes underneath it, haul it out and wash it down. Both animals took several minutes before they could move, because after being trapped in the mud for days their circulation had declined and they were unsteady on their feet. But after a few minutes they recovered, and the young rhino in particular showed his appreciation by charging his saviours and scattering everyone. Being a very small rhino, he could not run very fast and Phil ran ahead to encourage him to loosen his cramped muscles. After the rhino had had another go at Phil it ran off into the bush, squealing for its mother.

In the case of the baby elephant it refused to leave and tried to follow us back to camp. We stayed around the area hoping its mother would turn up. After a while a small group of elephants showed up and the baby elephant walked over towards them. The leading female of the group investigated the new recruit but immediately picked out the scent that we had left on him. She rapidly backed away. We watched to see if the group would eventually accept the infant. They turned and wandered down to a lagoon, with the young one trailing behind. They entered the lagoon and crossed it, walking off into the trees on the other side. Believe it or not, the baby elephant went and got stuck in the mud again trying to cross the lagoon with the others. So once again we set about digging. Again we waited for some elephant to turn up, and when they did, this time, we had to leave the young one and just hoped that it would be accepted by the group and survive.

By November the heat was appalling. It was desperately dry, 110° in the shade during the day and only dropping to 90° at night. I usually returned to the camp or parked for a few hours under a tree in the middle of the day. It was so hot that even the birds and animals found a shady place. The bush became quite dead during the heat of the day. Nearly all the small rivers, waterholes and lagoons were bone dry and cracked. One hundred miles north of my camp, above the point where two large rivers run into the Luangwa, the actual Luangwa itself ran dry, leaving pools at the bends in the river. Huge concentrations of hippos, five hundred strong in some places, could be found fighting for these deep pools. Long, savage fights would often occur as the hippos were forced virtually to live on top of each other. Dust and smoke filled the atmosphere, causing a heavy haze which made filming conditions quite difficult. Many animals, in particular the elephant, lost condition as their food supply rapidly diminished. One day I filmed a lone bull using his front foot to kick at the hard baked cracked soil, to hunt out tiny roots on which he was feeding. The amount he found would barely have kept a mouse alive, let alone an elephant. Backbones became far more prominent, and ribs began to show.

Finally, huge black heavy clouds began to appear on the horizon. But first the winds came, throwing up vast clouds of dust that could be seen for miles. When I returned to camp in the evening, my eyes were red and sore from the dust and heat. My hair and clothes were caked in dust, and worst of all, so were the cameras. Every night I had to clean them down completely getting all the dust, sand and grit out of them. When the rains did finally arrive in November, they would come with a huge clap of thunder, with lightning and high winds. Torrential rain descended on the parched valley. Within an hour small streams and gullies were bursting with raging water, small waterholes started to fill and roads became impassable. And then it would suddenly stop, and the water would slowly sink into the ground. Within two or three days new, green, lush grass would appear all over the valley. Another torrential storm lasting for a few hours, another good soaking over the valley, and more lush green grass would appear. After a few weeks of this, the rains would calm down and a steady downpour would continue, sometimes for days.

Chibembe Camp closed down and the tourists left in mid-November at the beginning of the heavy rains. A huge cleaning and clearing operation began, and the object was to store everything safely during the rains. I did not leave camp until the more gentle, steady rain began, and by then we had to struggle out of the valley.

When I arrived back in Lusaka the following February I learnt from friends and contacts that the rains had been unusually heavy and the Luangwa was very full. It had not broken its banks, but it was only inches from the top.

I needed one additional piece of equipment for the rains, a boat. Bill Barclay, as usual, came to my rescue. He had a jet-boat tucked away in a shed on his farm, so we got it out, cleaned out the cobwebs and mouse nests, and I towed it on a trailer down to the Kafue Dam for testing. I was also helped in re-establishing my camp in the Luangwa by Robin Pope, who was brilliant at improvisation, and Pat Gray a part-time professional hunter and trail-leader.

Once again I had Patterson looking after me. When I had sorted out my house by the lagoon, I went to see Pat and Robin to find out what had been going on.

The river was indeed full. But it had now fallen a few inches, below the top of the bank. Everything was lush and green, and there was new fresh grass everywhere. All the little streams, waterholes and lagoons were bursting, ditches and gullies flowing with turgid brown water. Debris floated down the river, logs, Nile cabbage and sometimes huge trees being tossed downstream, and finally grinding to a halt upside down with the roots in the air.

There was no longer the big concentrations of wildlife, the creatures had scattered all over the valley now that there was plenty of food. It was a good time for them. When it was not actually raining the sun was fierce and hot. All the dust and smoke in the air had settled. Visibility was good and for once I was able to drive to the top of a hill and see across from one side of the valley to the other.

I was not expecting to find many animals, as I thought that they had probably moved out to higher ground near the escarpment. But I was pleasantly surprised to find a few elephants, impala, puku, zebra, lions and baboons splashing about in the mud.

Our times out in the boat were the best, both for filming and for entertainment. Pat knew well the main river, the smaller rivers, and the entrances from the Luangwa into lagoons, and took me wherever the boat was able to go.

One morning we were driving upstream when we saw some way ahead a log floating down towards us. There appeared to be something lying on the log, we approached carefully. There lying on top was a huge crocodile, fast asleep, with its mouth wide open to show its horribly sharp, pointed teeth, and yellow throat. Pat cleverly guided the boat right up to the sleeping croc, while I filmed until we were within a few feet. I was about to tell him to clap his hands to make the croc wake up and slide into the water, when it obligingly did so.

Then it began to rain in earnest. A steady, heavy, continuous rain that went on for days and nights. It was, in fact, the beginning of the worst floods the Luangwa Valley had seen for fifty-one years. As each day of continuous rain passed, the tracks got worse. They became slippery and waterlogged. Huge ruts were cut out where the Land-Rover sank into the soft mud and I could only just struggle out.

But with the boat, life was more agreeable. The river started to rise, slowly at first. After the first three days of continuous rain, it rose three or four inches a day. Huge quantities of raging water began to pour into the river. The small rivers burst their banks, the lagoons spread out further and further with each passing day, and soon joined up with the river to form one mass of water. Raging torrents poured off the escarpment and rushed headlong across the valley floor, bursting their way into the Luangwa. Then the river rose even more, lapping over the top of the banks.

Still it rained and still the river rose. At the peak the Luangwa was rising about a foot a day, its banks disappeared and all the land was flooded. I was concerned for Pat and Robin in their camp right by the river, but we all presumed that the rain would stop and the floods, although they might spread out across the valley floor, would not get much deeper. But still it rained and the Luangwa rose, day after day.

One day we went out in the boat and found that where only a few days before trees and bushes had been growing right on the edge of the river, the ground had been cut away beneath them by the raging current and they had collapsed. After four miles we came across an amazing sight. Electric pylons carrying cables across the river had collapsed. The cables were lying in the river and floating debris, logs, bushes and trees were caught up. As more and more debris built up, the strain on the pylons still standing increased by the hour until they collapsed as well.

Pat sensibly decided to play safe and sent radio signals to the office in Lusaka to cancel all tourist bookings until the floods had finished.

Just before he left himself, I managed to get a radio message through to Bill Barclay in Lusaka to arrange for a high wing Cessna to fly up, so that I could get some aerial shots of the flooded valley. The escarpments were pouring millions of gallons of water into the valley, and the rivers were bursting over the banks. Their contents were all heading for the Luangwa, which was already bursting itself.

We flew along one of the rivers to where it finally flowed into the Luangwa. There was a large herd of buffalo wading in the floods. Two or three miles from the Luangwa, a bursting river split up into numerous small streams and flooded a large area miles wide. The lagoons were all overfull. Oxbow lagoons now connected up to the main river and extensive flooding could be seen everywhere. The whole place was under water.

Pat now told me that I must pull out myself. Part of the camp complex was three feet under water. All the tents were soaked, so we quickly unpegged the bottom part of the tents and folded them up into the fly sheets which were still above water. We could do nothing for any of the vehicles, there was just nowhere to go, so we left them. Mattresses, sheets, blankets and pillows were stripped off the beds and placed in one of the store houses amongst the roof beams. The kitchen and dining areas of the camp were two feet under water. The refrigerators and deep freezes were under water and not functioning. The gas cylinders were floating nearby. We heaved the equipment on to the dining-room tables, and tied the floating gas cylinders to poles. The dining-room chairs were hooked around the roof beams.

Robin decided that it was time to evacuate the camp staff as they were all complaining bitterly about the flooding in their huts. We began to ferry out all the men, women and children with their possessions. It took a whole day, working flat out in the pouring rain. The Game Department found accommodation for the staff, but Robin and Pat still refused to abandon camp. That night the Luangwa rose yet another foot, and next morning Robin got out of his bed and found himself standing up to his knees in water. That was it. He and Pat packed their suitcases and turned up at my house early in the morning.

For the next couple of days we salvaged as much of the camping equipment as possible. At midday we stopped to have a drink at the bar, mercifully the only place left above water. We were enjoying our drinks when suddenly we saw a huge twelve foot croc gently cruising through camp. That ended any further wading.

The effects of the floods on the wildlife were dramatic. Thousands of animals were caught. Some swam through the floods and landed on the built-up roads in the Park, where they had to stay for two or three weeks before the waters began to drop. Others were taken by crocodiles or drowned, eventually to be caught up in the bushes or trees. There were so many drowned animals about that the crocodiles were unable to cope. I saw numerous impala and puku standing right at the top of twenty foot anthills, totally surrounded by eight feet of water. There they had to stay until the floods subsided.

When it was possible we rescued animals, dragging them into the boat and setting them free on dry land. We came across a bush one day, only the last six inches of which was showing above the water. It was swarming with black ants desperately trying to find an escape route. Another time we came across a puff adder swimming through the water towards a bush which was its last refuge. Weaver nests, usually hanging from the branches of bushes and trees five or six feet above ground level, found themselves bobbing up and down in the water.

We went out every day in the boat, cruising gently through the wooded areas, always expecting to find a stranded lion or leopard in the trees. We never did. These animals must have kept ahead of the floods. We did find a poor elephant stranded on a tiny island. Luckily there were a few trees and bushes growing on the island on which the elephant was able to feed. On one side of the island was the raging Luangwa River, on the other a deep lagoon. The elephant walked up and down day after day trying to find a way out. It remained on that island for three very long wet weeks before the waters dropped enough for it to find a way to dry land.

All the hippos from the river moved out, the water was too deep for them. They waded out across the flooded areas until they found water not more than four feet deep. Eventually the rain stopped, yet still the Luangwa rose.

Although I had secured all the film I wanted, I could not yet leave the valley. There was no way out, not until the government repaired the broken roads and bridges, and that took another month.

One morning we went up the river in the boat. Some way ahead of us we could see a lot of splashing and a dark object appearing and disappearing in the water. I thought at first it was some crocodiles on a floating carcase, or maybe a large tree being tossed down river. It turned out to be a female elephant with a tiny baby calf, in mid-stream crossing the river. The female was in water forty feet deep, and she would go under for a few seconds and then reappear. Even her trunk, which she held up like a periscope occasionally disappeared under water. She blew like a whale each time she broke surface. The young calf was clinging to its mother's back, ears flapping, tiny trunk also held aloft, having the ducking of its life.

Elephants in deep water are helpless, so Pat and I were able to move in close with the boat. We stayed with them until they crossed. As soon as the cow reached the far bank she tried to climb out, but it was too steep and the water too deep for her to get any leverage. She slipped back into the river with her calf and they were swept downstream for thirty yards until she found a more suitable landing. With a lot of heaving and puffing and sliding in the mud, they both managed finally to scramble out.

It was not until early May that I received a message from one of the locals that temporary roads had been completed and I could now get through to Lusaka. That last evening I sat for several hours down by the river, which was sinking back to its normal level. Rather sadly I watched the sun set in a cloudless sky, and gazed at clumps of Nile cabbage and dead logs floating by. I heard hippos in the distance gently grunting, and watched several kinds of water birds flight across the setting sun. I sat and listened to the Luangwa River until darkness fell, and the beautiful picture in front of me faded into darkness.